SEEING STARS

Memoirs Of A Professional Celebrity—Seeker

EDWIN HOWARD

ROCKY RUN
PUBLISHING, LLC
MCLEAN, VIRGINIA

SEEING STARS

Memoirs Of A Professional
Celebrity—Seeker

ACKNOWLEDGEMENTS

In living, compiling, and finally writing "Seeing Stars," I am forever grateful, first, to the stars themselves – those happily still with us, and those who have gone on to that great movie screen in the sky. I am especially grateful to Dixie Carter, Hal Holbrook, Patricia Neal and author John Grisham for their friendship, and for sharing with me over a period of years their goals and accomplishments.

The unsung heroes of this book are the countless studio press representatives who over the years helped me gain access to the stars for my newspaper column, The Front Row. One of the first of these was A.C. Lyles, whose remarkable career began in the mail room at Paramount Studios, where he is now a producer, and included a stint in Washington on the presidential board of advisers for private sector initiatives to

President Ronald Reagan, who had been best man in Lyles' wedding. Another was the late Ralph Wheelwright, assistant studio publicity director for Metro-Goldwyn-Mayer for many years, who became my close friend, along with his wife Phinie and their children. Wheelwright was also the producer of "Blossoms in the Dust" and screenwriter of "Man of a Thousand Faces." Yet another top Hollywood press agent who has remained a valued friend is Jack Wiener, who turned producer with such films as "The Eagle Has Landed" and the cult classic, "F/X." The late Carl Ferrazza, of United Artists and Orion Films, put me in touch with numbers of stars, including Jack Nicholson, Paul Newman, and Martin Sheen. And Mac St. Johns, son of my dear friend, the late Adela Rogers St. Johns, did me many favors while he was at Columbia.

Among the many producers and directors who generously tolerated my presence on their sound stages and remote location sites, I want particularly to single out Howard Gottfried, producer of the late Paddy Chayefsky's film classics, "The Hospital" and "Network;" William Perlberg and George Seaton, producer and director, respectively, of "Teacher's Pet" and "The Counterfeit Traitor," and Stirling Silliphant, producer of "A Walk in the Spring Rain," who filmed it in my beloved Great Smoky Mountains after I suggested them to him. I am also deeply grateful to Directors Elia Kazan and the late James Bridges, about whom I have written more fully in the closing chapter of the book.

I also want to thank Paul Schumach of Bellmore, N.Y.; William Speer of Memphis, TN; Ed Frank and Jim Cole of the University of Memphis Libraries' Special Collections; and my longtime writer friend Joan Williams for their generous assistance with photographs.

I am deeply grateful to my publishers for their enthusiasm, persistence, and wise counsel, and to James and Andrew Rohrbach for highly valued technical assistance. I also wish to thank Edward Butera and IBI Designs, Inc., for their creativity and flexibility.

For their generosity in granting me, when I began working on the book eight years ago, permission to use material originally written while in their employ, I want especially to thank William R. Burleigh, then president and chief operating officer of Scripps-Howard, and Barney DuBois, then editor and publisher of the Memphis Business Journal.

Finally, I want to thank my daughters, Meg and Heather Howard, for crucial assistance when needed, and for enduring moral support. And most of all, I want to thank my wife Tugar, my first reader and best critic, who sat in on many of the interviews that led to this book, often contributing provocative questions, and always spreading her warmth and charm around me and whatever stars I was seeing at the time.

CONTENTS

INTRODUCTION

Who is this professional celebrity-seeker, and how did he get that way?

I began my newspaper career in August of 1942 as a copyboy on the staff of The Memphis Press-Scimitar. Two months later I was promoted to "beginning journalist," the American Newspaper Guild term for cub reporter. In the six months that remained before I was drafted into the Army in World War II, I covered every beat on the paper, and conducted my first two interviews with famous people. My subjects were Gen. Carlos P. Romulo, aide-de-camp to Gen. Douglas MacArthur, commander of U.S. forces in the Pacific, and Jan Christian Smuts, prime minister of the Union of South Africa.

Romulo had just won the Pulitzer Prize for journalism

for his reports on the military situation in the Pacific leading up to World War II. He and Smuts were both (but separately) touring the U.S. to rally Americans to the cause — in which we had been involved for less than a year — of defeating the Japanese and German war machines. Pretty heavy stuff for an 18-year-old cub reporter, but a great beginning for a 60-year career (so far) as a newspaper critic, columnist and interviewer.

Of all the hats I have worn in the newspaper business — and in the five years I spent as lively arts critic and celebrity interviewer on television — I have had the most fun under the broad brim of the interviewer's 10-gallon topper. Because? Well, when I have it on, I never know what's coming next.

For example: While In England in 1964 I located the widow of Col. Stewart F. Newcombe, commanding officer of the unit in which T. E. Lawrence won fame in the Arabian desert during World War I. Lawrence had been immortalized the previous year in David Lean's Academy Award-winning film masterpiece, "Lawrence of Arabia," starring Peter O'Toole.

Rose Newcombe invited me to tea at her home in Woodstock, near Oxford, and at what I thought was the propitious moment, I asked her what she thought of Lawrence. This, you understand, was at a time when "Lawrence of Arabia" and the true nature of Lawrence the man were favorite topics of conversation all over the world. Knowing that her husband had remained friends with Lawrence and that he had been a frequent visitor in their home between 1918 and Lawrence's death on a motorcycle in 1935, I eagerly awaited her evaluation of this enigmatic hero.

After a long, thoughtful pause and a sip of thick Turkish coffee, she replied with exquisitely precise emphasis: "Well, of

course, he was ONLY a leftenant on my husband's STAHFF."
I refrained from pointing out that history had made an
international hero of Lawrence, crediting him with successfully
leading the Arabs' revolt against Germany's troublesome allies,
the Turks.

In 1960, I covered the world premiere of "I Aim at the
Stars," the film bio of Wernher von Braun, the German rocket
scientist who built the Saturn rockets which nine years later
took the U.S. to the moon. While others crowded around von
Braun at the reception following the film, I joined his pretty
wife, Maria, at the buffet table. Amused at her husband's
sudden celebrity, she confided: "I told him the other day: 'You
want to go to the moon? Hell, you can't even hang a picture.'"

I had gradually gotten into celebrity interviewing when
I returned to The Press-Scimitar after two years in Italy and
Germany as an infantryman, then combat correspondent, and,
finally, co-founder and editor of the First Armored Division
newspaper, The Warrior. The interviewing was part of my job
as arts and entertainment editor of The Press-Scimitar, the
position I took on in 1946 and held until Scripps-Howard shut
the 102-year-old afternoon newspaper down in 1983.

Interviewing continued to be a big part of my job as
creator, editor and columnist of the Life at the Top section of
the Memphis Business Journal until it was sold in 1997. And
about once a year I work an interview into my arts and travel
columns for the Memphis monthly, The Best Times.

And just what is an interview exactly?

Well, it might be called biography in a hurry.
Newspaper interviews are usually biography in a terrible hurry,
producing not full-length portraits, but quick sketches.

The word comes from the Old French, entrevue, meaning "to see each other," or "face-to-face."

Sometimes seeing my subject was about all I was able to do. In 1951, for example, I was invited to the world premiere of Paramount's "Here Comes the Groom" at Bing Crosby's Elko, Nev., ranch. No interviews with Bing, though. Instead, a barbecue and a softball game between the press and Crosby's team, which included his sons Phillip, Dennis and Lindsay,

Bing Crosby chats up the author on the Crosby ranch in Elko, Nev., in 1951. (Author's collection)

Dorothy Lamour, Cass Daley, and sportscaster Ted Husing. Bing pitched with the wickedest wind-up since Satchel Paige. The final score was 23-22, but we never agreed which side won.

That same year during a visit to Hollywood, A.C. Lyles, who knew everybody who was anybody in Hollywood (and still turns up frequently as a resource on the A&E Channel's "Biography") introduced me to Ronald Reagan (soon to make a career change) on the set of "Hong Kong" at Paramount; to the legendary Cecil B. DeMille on the "Greatest Show on Earth" set, also at Paramount (and I swear C.B. was wearing jodhpurs and puttees); and to a 19-year-old beauty (with a 19-inch waist) named Elizabeth Taylor at the Egyptian Theatre's world premiere of MGM's "Go for Broke," a film about the Japanese-American 442nd U.S. Regimental Combat Team's extraordinary record in Italy during WWII.

Lots of face-to-face, but no real interviews yet.

Over at 20th Century-Fox I had better luck. My old friend and Knoxville, TN, schoolmate Patricia Neal was co-starring with Michael Rennie in "The Day the Earth Stood Still," and Pat was perfectly willing to sit still for a real interview. It was actually the second of the many interviews I would do with her over the years. (See Chapter 14: "Patricia Neal in the Valley of the Dahls.") The first had been in 1949 when she visited Memphis on a coast-to-coast tour with her debut film, "John Loves Mary," co-starring Ronald Reagan. (That guy sure got around.)

Though naturally shy, I gradually learned to speak up and, more important, to listen. My 1954 interview with a kid improbably named Elvis Presley, who when he started out was even shyer than I was, was the first print interview ever done

Ronald Reagan (left) welcomes author and his former wife, Olivia, to the set of "Hong Kong" at Paramount, 1951. (Author's collection)

C.B. DeMille greets author and then wife Olivia on the set of "The Greatest Show On Earth" in 1951. (Author's collection)

Elizabeth Taylor graciously poses with the author at a 1951 Hollywood movie premiere. (Author's collection)

with him (See Chapter 8: "Elvis: From the Beginning to the End"). It taught me that you never know where the next celebrity is going to come from.

From William Faulkner to John Grisham, I have learned much from the writers of our time, whose works I also reviewed for 30 years in The Press-Scimitar's Saturday Book Report, and Life at the Top's Books & Authors column.

I have always loved many kinds of music, and from Elvis to pianist Arthur Rubinstein, I have learned much about the artists who make it.

Having once thought, briefly, of becoming an actor myself, I have been fascinated, entertained, inspired and convulsed by some of the greatest actors of our time. The funniest interview I ever did was with Peter Sellers, whose Inspector Clouseau is one of the greatest comic creations in screen history. But alas, the interview was done for television, and falls rather flat in print.

I believe I can also lay claim to having interviewed the biggest and the smallest actors of our time. The biggest was Richard "Jaws" Kiel, who appeared in two James Bond films: "The Spy Who Loved Me" and "Moonraker." The smallest was surely Herve Villechaize, who starred in "The Gang That Couldn't Shoot Straight" and later became famous as Tattoo on the long-running TV series, "Fantasy Island."

The statistics?

Kiel stood 7 feet, 2 inches tall, weighed 330 pounds, and wore size 16EEE shoes.

Villechaize was 3 feet 10 inches short, and told me he never weighed over 70 pounds. He wore tiny cowboy boots and packed a switch-blade in the right one, to protect himself from

Richard "Jaws" Kiel, villain in two Bond films, was the biggest actor the author has interviewed. (Photo courtesy of Paul Schumach)

bullies who sometimes saw him as an easy mark.

The French-born midget (calling him a dwarf angered him) was a skilled painter and when gallery-owner friends of mine in Memphis next staged their "World's Smallest Arts Festival," I secured a small grant to bring him back to Memphis as its guest artist. He was delighted when they built him a miniature display cart and billed him as "The World's Smallest Artist."

The actor who affected me most deeply and enduringly was far from the best actor I have interviewed. Audie Murphy was a freckle-faced young fellow of 24 — exactly my age — when I interviewed him in 1949 in connection with the Southern premiere of his first starring film, "Bad Boy."

He looked and sounded so boyish that you would have expected to pull back damp fingers if you had touched him behind the ears. It seemed incredible that he had become the most-decorated hero of World War II by killing, wounding or capturing 240 German soldiers. He had been wounded three times himself, and been awarded 24 decorations for valor, including the Congressional Medal of Honor and four French decorations. (All this was later dramatized in the film version of his autobiography, "To Hell and Back.")

In person, Audie was matter-of-fact about his war record. "Bravery," he told me with an engaging grin, "is just a determination to do a job you know has to be done." I felt a special affinity for him, having served with no distinction whatever in several of the places he fought with the Third Division in Italy — notably the Anzio Beachhead.

Audie and I are separated today by no more than three or four miles, and the Potomac River. I'm in downtown

Washington, D.C., and he lies in a modest grave at the top of Arlington National Cemetery. He died on Memorial Day eve in 1971 in the wreck of an Aero Commander plane on Brushy Mountain near Roanoke, Va. He had recently completed his last film, "A Time for Dying."

I go over to Arlington to visit him from time to time and repeat what I told him that night in 1949 in the Variety Club bar in the old Hotel Gayoso in Memphis: "It sure was good having you around, Audie." For different reasons, I could say that to the other celebrities whose interviews I've assembled in this volume. Hope you enjoy reading about them as much as I enjoyed seeking them out.

Chapter 1

Mae West Invites Me Up To See Her

I t was in July, 1969, about the time our astronauts were making the first landing on the moon, that Mae West invited me to come up and see her in the Ravenswood Apartments suite where she had lived since the day she first arrived in Hollywood in 1931.

It was one of the two or three most extraordinary interviews I have had in 50 years of celebrity-interviewing — so extraordinary that I am only now emboldened to print the most intimate part of what she told me about herself. But first, here is the way I remember that memorable day:

☆ ☆ ☆

My appointment was for 4 p.m., but since I was going to interview a living legend I didn't want to risk being late. I arrived at the sedate Ravenswood Apartments on Rossmore, at the foot of fabled Vine Street in Hollywood, 10 minutes before the hour and asked the concierge to announce me.

"Miss West says she has company, and would you mind waiting about 15 minutes," he told me a moment later. I said I'd be glad to, I knew I was early, and sat down in the airy, high-ceilinged, baroque-furnished lobby to wait. The interview had been arranged for me by Stanley Musgrove, a cousin of novelist Jesse Hill Ford and an associate of producer/director Robert Wise. Musgrove and Wise were planning an hour-long TV special starring Mae for the coming winter.

I checked my tape recorder, jotting down a few questions I didn't want to forget, and felt like Cary Grant waiting to be admitted by Mae's maid Beulah in a 1930s movie. It had been 25 years since Mae West had made her last movie. She admitted to 76 years; the dictionary (yes, the dictionary; it lists her in defining the inflatable lifejacket named for her during World War II) says she was born Aug. 17, 1892, which would have made her 77; a man close to her told me she was actually 81. It has been said that she saved Hollywood in the Depression and that she was singlehandedly responsible for the adoption of the movie industry's self-censoring Production Code. If she didn't invent sex, she certainly popularized it in our century; when she wrote and starred in a play called "Sex" in 1925, the New York newspapers refused to publish the title in advertisements.

As I sat waiting for the word from Mae West to

come up and see her, a tall, dark man in a white suit followed by a boy of 10 or 11 entered the lobby. The man went to the concierge desk, said, "Tell Miss West I'm coming up," and led the boy into the elevator. From Musgrove's description at dinner a few nights before, I recognized the man as Leroy Jenkins, faith healer.

At five after 4, I asked the concierge to check again with Miss West. She said she still had company, and would I mind waiting 15 more minutes, but five minutes after that she called to say I should come on up.

A young man slipped the bolt on the door without using its speak-easy peep-hole and ushered me into the living room. The room was done in early Hollywood boudoir. Everything was off-white, pinkish beige and gold. A beige-toned mirror covered one wall. On the white baby grand piano stood Gladys Lewis Bush's white marble statue of Mae in the nude — Venus de Milo with arms. Over one of the two white sofas hung Florence Kinzell's oval-framed nude painting of Mae, rosily receptive on a chaise longue. Beige satin pillows edged in antique lace nestled in the corners of the sofas. Silver and gold-framed photos of the actress marched across the coffee table. An open box of Whitman Sampler on the piano sweetened the authentic '30s tableau.

Then, walking toward me and extending her hand from the folds of a simple white robe, its high, zippered neck caressed by a shower of platinum hair, was the living legend herself.

"Hello. I'm so glad you could come. Sorry to keep you waitin', but I had all these fellas here. Maybe you could just interview us all."

From a white satin straight chair in the center of

the room, to which she now returned, Mae West was holding court. (This was the Louis XIV chair in which she died 11 years later.) "I've lived here since the day I arrived in Hollywood," she told me. "I told the studio, 'Send me over a couple o' decorators. I want everything Louis the 14th.'" I recognized Jenkins, whose white suit, shirt and tie blended perfectly with the room's decor; his son, and composer/singer Jimmy Rogers. The young man who had admitted me was a friend of Jimmy's. They all sat there looking at me as I tried to get the interview going.

"Do you mind if I use my tape recorder?" I asked Mae. "Oh. Well, I'd rather you didn't. Those things inhibit me. I don't even like to use 'em when I write. I can't create if I have any distractions."

Of course my first question had to be about the then current sex explosion on Broadway and in films.

"If they keep it up," she said, "it's just gonna be repetitious. Nudity has a certain audience — the same percentage as burlesque, and how long is that going to last? Of course, it all started in 1925 with my play, 'Sex.' I had to go to jail for that one, but they didn't get around to arresting me till two years after it opened. That was because by then everybody else was doin' it. I got 10 days but they gave me two days off for good behavior.

"They're ready for 'Sex' now. I was just ahead of the time. I did another play called 'The Drag' in New Jersey in 1927. I had six gay boys in it and they came out from New York and begged me not to take it to Broadway. Said it would upset people and they wouldn't be able to handle it. They're interested in that now — you know, the homosexual theme. I

The Ravenswood Apartments, Mae West's home from her arrival in Hollywood in 1931 to her death, at 89, in 1980. (Author's collection)

got $20 a seat for that one and $10 a seat for 'Sex' and that was a time when Ziegfeld was only gettin' $6 a seat for the Follies.

"The kinda thing they're doin' now had to come, but it'll go just like it came, see? It goes right back to the play's the thing. You've got to get back to entertainment."

I asked her what she would do on her TV special.

"Some of the things I usually do," she said. "I won't disappoint my audience. I'll have Leroy on (the part-American-Indian faith healer and singer beamed) — mostly men. That's what I'm used to."

Leroy stood up to fill me in on his recording career.

"My album, 'Songs and Sermons by Leroy Jenkins,' has sold 800,000 copies," he said, "and 'Songs in the Night' has sold 1,300,000."

With that insinuating twinkle in her eye that hints at meanings beyond her words, Mae said, "Maybe you ought to interview Leroy. Now that's a real story. He heals people. I saw him put his hand on this man's vocal cords. He hadn't spoken in 30 years, and Leroy put his hand on him and he spoke. . ."

Leroy grinned and said, "But I can't do anything with Mae. I told my congregation I'd try to save 'er, but she's as bad as ever."

Mae looked him up and then looked him down again and said: "When she's good she's very very good, but when she's bad, she's better."

Mae doesn't mind quoting herself (she wrote the line for "I'm No Angel") when it fits the occasion.

We talked about her movies and her leading men.

"'She Done Him Wrong' and 'I'm No Angel' saved Paramount," she said. "They had 1,700 theatres and they were about to lose 'em when I came along. I put Cary Grant in my first picture. Saw 'im at the studio and made 'im my leading man, see. I guess he's still my favorite. I liked 'im so well I had 'im twice."

Jimmy Rogers and his friend were talking between themselves now, and with a broad smile Mae said: "Would you boys like to go into the other room to discuss your business?"

"No, Mae," Jimmy said. "That's O.K. We're fine right here."

Still smiling, Mae said: "I mean if you need to talk, I'd rather you'd go in the other room." They listened quietly for another 15 minutes or so and then left. Meanwhile, Mae had gotten two phone calls from a man in the lobby — a friend of Leroy's — who wanted to come up and see her right away.

She had refused to take the first call, then asked Leroy to take the second.

"He's got some material he thinks'd be good for your special, Mae," Leroy said. "I told him you're busy but he wants to come up. He's tryin' to help you."

Mae paused for two beats and spread that double-entendre smile across her famous features again. "He can't be any help here now," she said. "When I already got five men here (she graciously included Leroy's young son in the sweep of her hand), what can HE do?"

After Rogers and his friend left, Mae asked Leroy how the singer/composer was getting along, referring to an incident in which Rogers had been mysteriously hit over the head about a year ago.

"He's a whole lot better," Leroy said, "But he still has those spells sometimes and he's got the arth-a-ritis somethin' terrible."

"Well, Leroy," Mae said with serious concern, "Why don't you give 'im a healin'?"

"I'm goin' to," Leroy told her, "just as soon as I can get him by himself. You know I KNEW he was gonna get hit on the head. I tried to warn 'im, but it was too late."

While Mae bade Leroy and his son a long farewell at the door, I tried to separate the Mae West character from the actress. I couldn't. Maybe, I thought, playing the role of the perennial sexpot had kept her so young. There were lines around her mouth and neck, but I'd seen women of 55 or 60 who looked older. Her flesh was still firm and clear, as I remarked to her later, and though she looked shorter than she did on the screen, her figure was still Junoesque. Her eyes sparkled with life and humor, and her conversation was sprinkled with both spontaneous and recycled wit. The most surprising things about her were a childlike immodesty about her accomplishments and appearance — almost as if she were talking about someone else — and a wide-eyed faith in Leroy's healing powers.

When she came back, apologizing, into the room, she explained: "Leroy is having trouble with some of his people. He's got a staff of a hundred, see, and some of 'em are tryin' to tell him what to do. I've been through all that and I was tellin' 'im he'd have to get rid of em.

"He's really got the power, you know. It came to him eight years ago when he almost died. He was puttin' in a 250-pound piece of plate glass and it fell, cut 'im so bad his right arm was hangin' by a sinew. He told his brother, 'Don't let 'em take my arm, I'd rather be dead.' They said they'd have to amputate, but his brother wouldn't let 'em.

"He went outside his body and saw them sewin' his arm back on. If you know ESP, you can do that. They said he was dead, but his brother wouldn't let 'em take him away. That's when God gave 'im the power. He said, 'Use that hand to heal,' and Leroy came back in his body and started breathin' again and he's been healin' ever since."

I was listening, but I was also looking at Mae's hands, and couldn't resist remarking on the firmness and clarity of the skin that covered them.

"Yeah," she smiled, eyes twinkling as she admired her own hands. "Well, that's me all over.

"My doctor comes in and checks me over and he says, 'Mmmm! Eighteen!' I'm very fortunate in that I never had children. I never wanted any. I was never even — that way. Maybe I just didn't meet the right man. (She was married once, in 1911, to vaudeville hoofer Frank Wallace, but in a divorce hearing 30 years later testified that the marriage was never consummated.) I always wanted to be the baby."

"How DO you keep so youthful, Mae?" I asked, and, very seriously, she told me:

"Well, I don't drink and I don't smoke, and I never did. I can't stand to be around people who smoke. My father was an athlete. We had a gym and it was health, health, health all the time. Watching my food — never any candy — was part of my training.

"Then in 1959 I found out something about myself that's part of the secret. I was in Las Vegas with my Muscle Men, and my hairdresser gave me a virus. I had 'im use a surgical mask, but I got it anyway. My doctor said, have your chest X-rayed in case there's a little pneumonia there.

"Well, they saw something on the X-ray, see, and they didn't know what it was, so they called in experts, and this doctor said, 'Miss West, you've got a double thyroid.'

"I said, 'Oh my God!'

"But he said, 'Don't worry. Everybody should have two thyroids.' And he said it explains a lot of my tremendous energy. You know, it's a little gland, shaped just like a policeman's badge, and it controls the sex and everything."

"Isn't that unusual," I straight-manned it, "having two of them?"

She drew herself up with what may or may not have been mock pride, and said, "My doctor says only one in 10 million have it."

But she doesn't give her double thyroid all the credit for her youthful appearance and feelings.

"The main thing," she added confidentially, "is to keep your insides clean. You got to keep your kidneys and liver young. If not, it shows in your face. It says in the Bible they lived to be 900 years old. I bet they didn't show it."

She then went on to tell me, in considerable detail, some other secrets of her youthfulness, secrets she intended to describe "in a medical way" some day in a book but which she felt could not be properly discussed in a newspaper. I promised to respect her confidence.

Before I left, she filled me in on other career activities. Twentieth-Fox had called again that day to urge her to play a talent agent, Letisha Van Allen, in the film version of "Myra Breckenridge" and money was all that was keeping them apart. (The next week, she signed to do the role, for which she was to be billed over Raquel Welch in the title role, for reportedly more money.) Warner Bros.-Seven Arts and Mervyn LeRoy were also dickering with her, she said, for "Sextette," a play she wrote in 1961 and tried out in Palm Beach and Columbus, Ohio. There was also interest, she said, in a film version of her 1925 shocker, "Sex."

As she rose to see me to the door three hours after our interview began, I remarked that although she was not as tall as she appeared on the screen, neither was she as short as I had been told.

"I think I'm a nice size." she said. "I'm about 5-6 in my heels. Of course I always looked taller because I have a very full figure. (She outlined her bosom with her hands.) I'm very full up here. I'm all bound in now. If I weren't (she moved her hands forward) I'd be out to here."

Mae West the legend and Mae West the living, I decided going down in the elevator, were quite inseparable.

☆   ☆   ☆

"Myra Breckenridge," released in 1971, and "Sextette," released in 1978, were both box office bombs, and Mae West never appeared professionally again. She did manage to get her autobiography published before her death in 1980, so I now feel free to write about the health secrets she revealed to me that day in 1969.

After telling me the importance of "keeping your insides clean," she confided that she took "regular high colonics," meaning high colonic irrigation. In addition to that, she said, she had experimented with different diets for years, finally settling on a diet of fruit as the healthiest and most satisfactory for her.

"And I want to tell ya," she added delicately, lowering her voice, as we stood together in a small anteroom away from her other guests, "It's the cleanest diet you can have. My feces smell just like flowers."

Earlier, when she handed me a color transparency of herself to run with my interview, she said, "Now be sure and tell 'em this picture was made this month — in July, 1969. If there are shadows around my neck, you might get it retouched a little. I never had my face lifted, see; never needed it except right there sometimes if I didn't hold my chin up." So when Mae died at 92, or 89, or whatever, sitting up in her white Louis XIV chair, I was sure that this first and greatest sex goddess of our century had kept her body healthy, and clean, and her face unlifted to the very end.

Chapter 2

Cary Grant Gives Me An Acting Lesson

When I met Cary Grant in 1957, I needed reassurance. I had just seen myself on-screen in a scene from the Doris Day/Clark Gable comedy, "Teacher's Pet," then in production at Paramount. The studio had flown half a hundred real-life newspaper people like me to Hollywood to play the fictional newspaper people presided over by Gable as managing editor of the film's "New York Chronicle." A few of us had been thrown a line or two of dialogue. I had just seen the rushes of mine, and was still in shock the day I was introduced to Grant on the set of "Kiss Them for Me," co-starring newcomer Suzy Parker.

It's hard to describe the pain and suffering of seeing yourself on the big motion picture screen for the first time. But a few days later, I tried to describe it to Cary Grant. I told him I was sure I didn't slouch when I walked the way the representation of me on the screen did. My shoulders didn't slump that way. My nose wasn't that crooked, and I certainly didn't have a double chin, even when I looked down.

It got worse, I told him. The monster spoke. I was sure that voice had come from somebody else. That mushmouthed drawl couldn't possibly be mine. I have eliminated all but a pleasant hint of a Southern accent. Elvis had just finished filming "Loving You;" maybe they had accidentally dubbed in his speaking voice for mine, thankuver'much.

Grant assured me that my reaction to seeing myself on the screen was utterly typical.

I was questioning him about his amazing ability to fix other actors in scenes with him, or the camera itself, with an unblinking stare, and hold that fixed stare through an entire scene, moving his face, perhaps, but never his eyes.

He warmed to the subject at once, fixing ME with the stare under discussion and talking with that fascinating between-the-teeth delivery of his.

"What most people don't realize," he said, "is that if they move a couple of inches in front of that camera, they will have moved 20 feet on the theatre screen.

"Most people see themselves on the screen for the first time, and, like you, are horrified. Even a professional actor sees his first screen test and his reaction is: 'That can't be me! I've got to camouflage myself.' So next time he gets in front of a camera he starts trying to act. He mumbles or affects an accent, or picks his nose, or scratches under his arm, and comforts himself that although he may still be awful, at least people will think it's because he's acting.

"And judging from the awards some of the mumble-

and-scratch school of actors get, a lot of people do."

Then Cary Grant confided to me the simple secret of being great — or at least not utterly awful — on the motion picture screen.

"The really great movie stars," he said with that twinkling smile of his, "are those who can look at themselves on the screen and be satisfied with what they see. This sounds like conceit, but it isn't. It is simply the reflection of a kind of inner calm.

"Of course, it is a very rare quality, this willingness to stand inspection by the camera. Very few people are satisfied with themselves, off-screen or on. They hide behind cigarette-holders, or fans, or pipes, or silly giggles.

"It takes courage to be yourself, but the really great stars have had it. It's what Gary Cooper has. Grace had it. (Grace Kelly, with whom he starred in 'To Catch a Thief'). Sophia has it. (He would soon be seen with Sophia Loren in 'The Pride and the Passion.')

"Suzy Parker there has it to an amazing degree for a newcomer to the screen. She has been a very successful model, of course, but she's never had any professional acting experience. Yet she has such calm and contentment that she is utterly herself when she acts — and completely oblivious of the camera."

All of this didn't make me any more content with my scene in "Teacher's Pet," but it sure made me more content to be what I really was — a newspaperman lucky enough to have access from time to time to such wise and gifted people as Cary Grant.

☆ ☆ ☆

Twenty-nine years later, in Grant's 82nd year, I encountered him again. This time, the setting was the stage of the Orpheum Theatre in Memphis. He was touring his one-man show, "An Evening With Cary Grant," and I was covering it for my Life at the Top arts and leisure section of the Memphis Business Journal.

The question-and-answer format he had devised resulted in what might be called a mass interview.

What made the evening memorable was not so much the things he said, but the way he said them. Behind every polite and smiling answer to every routine or vapid or fawning question from the audience was the vague suspicion that he just might tell the next person who asked a really stupid question that it WAS a really stupid question.

He never actually did it, because he was a gentleman, but there was in many of his answers that duality which made him one of the two or three best film actors who ever were. It was this ambiguity — the darkness, the hint of malice, beneath the debonair manner — that made Hitchcock films like "Notorious" and "Suspicion" and "To Catch a Thief" work, and kept all those Howard Hawks comedies like "Bringing Up Baby," "His Girl Friday" and "I Was a Male War Bride" from getting either ridiculous or boring.

The playfulness always had an edge to it. The teasing could be merciless — and that hint of cynicism was still there on the stage as he half-sat and half-crouched on a stool in front of a microphone for two hours and answered questions about his career.

The most interesting thing about the questions was not what was asked, but what wasn't.

Cary Grant inscribed his name in forecourt of Grauman's (now Mann's) Chinese Theatre in 1951. (Author's collection)

Nobody asked if he really fell desperately in love with Sophia Loren and asked her to marry him as she said in her book. Nobody asked what it was like to be married to Woolworth heiress Barbara Hutton. Nobody seemed to want to know why he broke up with Dyan Cannon, mother of his only child, Jennifer.

There finally was one question about the 20-year-old Jennifer — something circumspect like, "Tell us about Jennifer." With obvious fatherly pride, he called her "the best production I ever made" and said: "She goes to Stanford and is now spending a semester at sea aboard the SS Universe. They're going around the world with some wonderful professors, learning about the countries they visit."

Although Grant had begun by inviting the audience to

Clark Gable, as the tough managing editor in 1957's "Teacher's Pet" (and suitor to Doris Day) gives an assignment to the author, playing one of his reporters in the movie. (Author's collection)

"ask me anything," I think the reason nobody asked gossipy questions was that he never gossiped himself. He never ever kissed and told, and I think everybody knew he wasn't about to do it that night.

Asked if he ever planned to write a book about his life and career, he said, "I wouldn't think of it. I deplore that sort of thing. I don't think anyone can tell the truth about themselves because they don't know it."

Of books that had been written about him, he said that only Richard Schickel's is "fairly accurate." In the others, he said, "they say I'm a homosexual, I'm a miser.... They make up anything. They're all just out to make a buck. But," he added with a disarming smile, "what can you do?"

Most of the women in the audience who raised their hands to ask questions prefaced them by informing the actor that they had been in love with him since "The Philadelphia Story" or "Indiscreet," or whatever film they had first seen him in. Although Grant was 82, he still looked about 60, and the women who were "in love" with him ranged down to an apparent 20 or 25.

Asked, inevitably, by one audience member to name his "favorite" leading lady, he said he didn't have one. "I loved them all — Ingrid, Audrey, Kate. But if you ask me who was the best actress, I'll tell you. It was Grace Kelly. She had an enormous gift for relaxation. When she played a scene with me, she was actually talking to me and listening to me. I know she was listening because sometimes I changed the words and it didn't throw her. She was never wondering what she looked like on camera."

When a film student tried to get him to compare the directorial techniques of Howard Hawks and Alfred Hitchcock, Grant said, "I don't want to disabuse you of your theories and your thoughts, but we just said what we were supposed to say and avoided bumping into each other."

He talked a lot about comedy: "It's much easier to make people cry than to make them laugh.... Nothing is so immediately apparent as the failure of a comedy. If you don't hear laughter, it's a flop. In a drama, they just sit quietly and you can't tell how they're reacting."

Grant said George Burns, as a former straight man for his wife Gracie Allen, had the best understanding of comedy of anybody he knew, and the best sense of timing.

Why did Grant quit films after "Walk Don't Run" in 1966?

"I had done it," he said. "I was tired of it, frankly. I had actually quit more than a dozen years before and spent a couple of years traveling around the world. Then Hitch called me back to make 'To Catch a Thief' and I got caught up in the career thing again."

The silver-haired actor told a number of stories about specific films. For example, he said that in "The Philadelphia Story" he really did push Katharine Hepburn in the face, though she landed on a mattress out of view of the camera. He said he had persuaded writer-producer Joe Mankiewicz to write the scene into the script to avenge a scene, years earlier in "Sylvia Scarlett," in which Hepburn hit him, and hit him really hard, and he warned her he would one day get even. "But I love Kate," he concluded, "and always have."

By the time his sense of timing told him the evening was over, Grant had committed himself to the audience just as fully as he always committed himself to the camera — honestly, without disguise or deception, looking it straight in the eye, and having the courage to be himself.

As he got up to bid the audience goodnight, he introduced — with his own distinctive brand of urbanity and charm — his fifth wife, Barbara Harris, an English publicist whom he had married five years before.

He was still so handsome, so charming, and in such apparent good health at the age of 82 that it was a terrible shock when, on Nov. 29, 1986 — just a few weeks and cities down the road — I read that he had died of a heart attack.

Chapter 3

SOPHIA LOREN: SHE CAN COOK, TOO

The first time I saw Sophia Loren face to face was in May of 1957, which, though it was not common knowledge then, was her Cary Grant year — the year their first film together, Stanley Kramer's bloated Spanish epic, "The Pride and the Passion," in which she co-starred with Grant and Frank Sinatra, was released; the year she made perhaps her best Hollywood film, "Houseboat," with Grant; and the year he fell desperately in love with her and asked her to marry him.

Under the circumstances, who wouldn't have?

She was 22 years old, warm, unaffected, and a proud, statuesque 5 feet 8 inches tall, with an incredible body measuring 38-23-35 in the most popular places.

The outlines of those places were already familiar to American movie audiences, thanks to her first film released by an American studio, "Boy on a Dolphin." Through much of the film, in which she played a native Greek diver hired to help find and raise from the bottom of the Aegean Sea the film's eponymous sculpture, director Jean Negulesco kept her gorgeous, scantily clad form revealingly wet down. I've always thought that those scenes were the inspiration, a few years later, for the first wet T-shirt contests in Ft. Lauderdale, Fla.

With her nipples pointing the way to fame and fortune in hundreds of American newspapers and magazines, Sophia was signed by Paramount to co-star with Burl Ives and Anthony Perkins in a film version of Eugene O'Neill's "Desire Under the Elms."

I happened to be in Hollywood, and working at Paramount as an extra in "Teacher's Pet," at exactly the time she arrived there for the first time to begin filming "Desire."

One day, all of us extras were invited to a mass press conference with Sophia Loren in her cottage dressing-room.

All I remember about that event is the star's mesmerizing glamour and irresistible natural charm; I did not bother recording anything that was said. I was so busy looking that I doubt if I heard anything that was said.

Besides, I was already angling for a private one-on-one interview. Director George Seaton had asked me, along with several others, if I would be interested in staying over a second week to do some lines in the film. This gave me time to set up my interview with Sophia.

It was scheduled for the following Tuesday when she would be posing for a portfolio of publicity pictures. I could hardly wait — and, as it turned out, I didn't have to.

On Sunday morning, I went into the pharmacy in the

Sophia Loren, in 1957, shows the author how tall she was when (he hopes) she was among the children to whom he, along with other U.S. soldiers, gave candy on Naples' docks in 1944. (Author's collection)

Beverly Hilton Hotel, where we "Teacher's Pets" were billeted. There was inexhaustible, irrepressible Sophia, doing a photo layout for Look Magazine. Mesmerized again, I stood watching her fall easily and uncomplainingly into whatever pose the photographer wanted when suddenly our eyes met.

"Hi!" she said. "I know you. You were in my dressing-room the other day."

Sophia Loren recognized me — remembered me! This woman was clearly going to become a great star. We chatted briefly, and I told her I was looking forward to our interview on Tuesday. She told me she was, too, and made me believe she meant it.

Two long days later, Loren talked volubly between publicity shots on any subject I brought up, from the possibility that I might have been one of the GIs who kept her from starving with chocolate bars in Pozzuoli, Italy, in 1944, to popular American music, cooking, and men.

In the gold lamé, off-one-shoulder gown she was wearing, Sophia looked not at all like the skinny starveling she had been at the age of 9, when the Allies used the Naples suburb where she was waiting out the war with relatives as a staging area for the Anzio Beachhead landings.

And she did credit the soldiers' generosity with keeping her alive.

"I was about this tall," she said, holding her hand out at shoulder height, "and so skinny they called me 'stecchito' — little stick."

I desperately wanted to believe that I had helped save this magnificent specimen of feminity from starvation, and she was kind enough to say that I might have done just that. What she actually said was:

"All the soldiers gave me candy. If you were there, maybe you did, too."

Sophia was playing Al Hibler's "Sweet Slumber" on her

record player to keep herself in the mood for the portrait session. She said he and Ella Fitzgerald were her favorite American singers, but she had seen Lena Horne on television a few nights earlier, and was still excited about her. Rolling her big expressive eyes, she exclaimed in her slight but irresistible Italian accent: "Oohhhsz! She had me scrimming!"

As for Elvis Presley, who was in Hollywood making his third film, she said apologetically that she hadn't heard him yet.

When I asked the old inevitable — What do you think of American men? — she pursed her lips, tilted her head, and said, in a fair approximation of an English accent: "They're proper smashing!" Then, with another roll of her enormous green eyes: "Wow! I dig them!"

The sensational Italian star said she loved Hollywood and what she'd seen of the rest of the country; said she would like to live in America. The only thing she didn't like was American food.

"What I've got," she said, "I got from spaghetti, but I can't find good spaghetti in America."

It seemed the right time to ask another inevitable question: Did she cook, too? Loren fixed me with a 1,000-watt gaze, narrowed her eyes almost ecstatically, and sort of moaned, "Oooohh, yes!" Then she added, with Academy Award emotion, "And I love to!" All that, and cooking, too. It was almost more than a man could stand.

☆ ☆ ☆

Three years later, I interviewed Loren again — this time in her Paris apartment, thanks to my friend Jack Wiener, now a

Hollywood producer but then Columbia's vice president for publicity and promotions in Europe.

Later in 1957, the actress had married her discoverer and first producer, Carlo Ponti, the man she had first met when he judged a beauty contest she entered at 14 — and lost; the man for whom she had turned down Cary Grant. However, Italian law did not recognize Ponti's Mexican divorce from his estranged wife and they could have been jailed for bigamy in their own country. In 1962, they had the marriage annulled. Then, after four more frustrating years, they took out French citizenship and remarried, and Sophia produced her handsome son, Carlo Ponti Jr., who as a baby made a brief screen appearance with her in "Sunflower" in 1970 .

In February of 1960, when, at Wiener's behest, she invited me to her Paris apartment on the rue de Rivoli, Loren was in the midst of the most productive period in her entire career. She had just finished three films — "Heller in Pink Tights" with Anthony Quinn for George Cukor, "It Started in Naples" with Clark Gable, and "A Breath of Scandal" with Maurice Chevalier — and was about to star in two more, bringing her 1960 releases to five. The film she was about to make in Rome, risking arrest, was "Two Women," which won her the Academy Award and recognition as a superb actress as well as a great beauty. And it was followed by the title role in Anthony Asquith's English production of G.B. Shaw's "The Millionairess," which stood in stunning contrast to her "Two Women" role.

In the three years since our first meeting, Sophia, at 25, had matured and grown reflective — and, on this day, melancholy.

☆ ☆ ☆

It was a gray day in Paris. Mist curled about the bare trees in the Tuileries as busy teachers herded long lines of pupils across the rue de Rivoli.

From a window overlooking the street and the sweeping gardens, a striking face with huge almond eyes stared up toward the Place de la Concorde, back toward the Louvre, then out across the gardens, with their precise rows of trees, toward the Seine.

"Marie Antoinette," Loren said as she stared, "looked out a window at those gardens the day she died."

She turned back toward the room, and her mood seemed to change as she asked, "Did you see Norma Shearer in Marie Antoinette? I never liked her very much. But I liked that picture." (Ed. note: I learned later from her autobiography, "Sophia — Living and Loving: Her Own Story (1979)," that Sophia's mother had won a Norma Shearer look-alike contest in Italy, held in connection with the release of "Marie Antoinette.")

It was as if in talking of a motion picture, the tall, intense young actress were returning to reality. And indeed movies had been her reality for at least the past four years.

"And another movie I liked — I must have seen it four or five times — was that one with Merle Oberon and Laurence Olivier. What was its name? You know the one where she kept calling (and here she cupped her hands to her mouth): 'Heathcliff! Heathcliff!'

"Oh — 'Wuthering Heights.' Yes, that's the one. What

an actor, that Olivier. He is not normal, you know — he is a genius. I would like to make a picture with him some time. And with William Wyler (who directed "Wuthering Heights"). He is a fine director, I think.

"Vittorio de Sica is going to direct again for the first time in three years when I make Alberto Moravia's 'Two Women' this summer in Rome. I have great faith in that man. I was almost born with him, you know. My first picture, 'Gold of Naples,' was for him. He is almost Neapolitan, like me. We understand each other."

She sat down in a high-backed chair, less interested, seemingly, as she spoke of the three films she had completed in the past year in Hollywood, Paris, Vienna and Naples. How did she feel, I wondered, about staying only a few weeks or months in one place, then moving on to another?

Loren arose, lighted a cigarette, walked restlessly around the room for a moment, the faded blue jeans she wore beneath a short-sleeved red sweater a strange contrast to the rich velvets and brocades of the ornately furnished, high-ceilinged living-room of her apartment. Still, it would have been hard to say which was the more elegant.

Abruptly she sat down on the sofa, tucking her feet beneath her and hugging her knees.

"For four years," she sighed, "I have been like a gypsy — always traveling, always working. In those four years I have made — let me see — 11 pictures. Sometimes you think it is going to drive you mad. Crazy, you know? You have no stability, always moving around.

"So now I have not worked since I finished 'It Started in Naples' in December. I have been here in Paris ever since then, trying to rest and relax. I won't work again until I start on 'Two Women' in June — unless I find another story I want to do in the meantime. But no! I don't think I will do it."

Suddenly she was arguing with herself.

"Why? It means only money, and after you have a certain amount, money does not mean so much any more.

"But I cannot relax here. I have been working the whole time. They call me up and they say, 'Please, Sophia, just this one newspaperman. See him for a few minutes. It will be very good publicity. And when I am in Paris, I cannot tell them no. I am here anyway, and I do not want to be unkind. So, at the end of the month, I am going to my farm in Bergenstock, Switzerland.

"I love Bergenstock. And they do not bother me there. If they try, I tell them to go to hell!

"Here in Paris I can't go outside. I can't go shopping. I can't do anything without people stopping and staring and gathering around. I like Paris, but it will be good to get away."

Is fame worth the price, then?

Her eyes seemed to give off sparks as she sat upright and answered without hesitation:

"Of course it's worth it. Happiness is to do what you like to do and be pleased with it. If you were happy all the time, you would not know what happiness was.

"To be bored is the only thing I cannot stand. There is no use to live if you are bored."

She walked back to the high window overlooking the Tuileries.

"You see?" she said, staring out again. "I am not complex. I am a very simple girl."

In the three years between my two interviews with her,

fame had transformed Sophia Loren from an excited, bubbling discovery — being wooed by one of the world's handsomest men, Cary Grant, as well as the major Hollywood studios — into an established star. Now married, yet legally a bigamist in her own country, her bubbling personality had turned melancholy, and she was already a bit jaded.

In a few more months, she would give her Oscar-winning performance in "Two Women." By the end of the decade, despite miscarriages, she would have fulfilled her dream of motherhood by stubbornly going to bed for nine months.

If she has never become the great actress this period in her career seemed to promise, the reason was the roles she played, not her performances in them. And she has nevertheless endured, becoming, if not a great actress, a very great lady.

Chapter 4

THE UNKNOWN JOHN WAYNE: LIBERAL, BALLETOMANE

John Wayne was the Grand Canyon of movie stars — bigger and ruggeder and a more enduring landmark than almost any other I have encountered in more than 50 years of interviewing celebrities. Like the Canyon walls, he had a lot of rough edges — but also like the Canyon, he was deeper than expected, as I found out one wild evening in 1975 at his beautiful bay-front home in Newport Beach, California.

I had first met Wayne in 1958 outside Natchitoches, La., on location for a film called "The Horse Soldiers." But he was too busy to talk to me beyond an exchange of pleasantries. He was not only co-starring in the Civil War film with William Holden; he was also learning to direct from his old friend and mentor, John Ford.

It was more than a decade later that I was able to have

my first real conversation with Wayne, in the course of the world premiere of "Chisum" in Dallas in 1970, a few months after he won his Oscar as Rooster Cogburn in "True Grit." Cornering the 6-foot-4-inch film legend at a pre-premiere barbecue at his friend Gordon McLendon's ranch outside Dallas, I got to ask him about his little-known career as Hollywood's first singing cowboy, and how he came by the nickname Duke.

Wayne, born Marion Michael Morrison in Winterset, Iowa, in 1907, got into the movies by way of football stardom at the University of Southern California. During summer vacations, he worked as a laborer and prop man, and eventually a stunt man, on the old Fox lot. There he was befriended by Ford, who started casting him in bit parts about 1928. He was such a big good-looking guy that Herbert Yates, the Republic Pictures boss, signed him as "Singing Sam," the first singing cowboy.

"Of course, I couldn't even carry a tune," Wayne told me, "so all my songs had to be dubbed. Finally, after several pictures, I went to Yates and told him I'd had it, to please get him a cowboy who could sing. And that's where Gene Autry came from."

Yates was also responsible for Wayne's acquiring his nickname, Duke, he told me.

"In those days," Wayne related, "every cowboy star had a horse he shared billing with. It was Tom Mix and Tony, Ken Maynard and Tarzan, and so on. Yates told me my horse had to have a name and asked me if I had any ideas.

"I said, well, I used to have a dog named Duke when I was a kid, and that sometimes people called me Duke, after

At the world premiere of "Chisum" in Dallas in 1970, John Wayne graciously posed with the author's daughter, Heather, then 12.
(Author's collection)

the dog."

So in his next picture, "Haunted Gold," in 1933, John Wayne shared star billing with a beautiful white horse named Duke. "Later," he concluded, "everybody gradually began calling me Duke, after the horse."

Wayne was as tough as he looked. In 1963 he had had a cancerous lung removed, so I asked him about his health. "I don't think I've let up much since the operation," he said. "I make about one and a half movies a year. Two is too many, but one isn't enough to keep you busy. I don't tire very easily. I can still hit the bottle pretty good when I feel like it. A belt of Who-Hit-John still tastes pretty good on a cold mornin'.

"Of course, I've had to let up on some things. I had to give up the cigarettes, but I only miss 'em now and then. I tell you: The only thing that's really bothered me since I quit smokin' is watchin' the Jackie Gleason Show. You know, when the girl brings out that cup of gin that's supposedly tea, and he gulps it and then takes that big, deep drag on that cigarette. That's when I really miss it."

He toughed out open-heart surgery in 1978, and had to have his stomach removed before he died in 1979. By that time, he had become a public figure, often ridiculed or reviled by the media for what was perceived as his extreme conservatism, and his hawkishness on the Vietnam War, which he idealized in his 1968 film, "The Green Berets."

One of the things that made my next encounter with Wayne — at his Newport Beach home in 1975 — so fascinating was hearing from his own lips that he considered himself a liberal. Another was watching and listening to him wax poetic over ballet — yes, ballet — and go into ecstasies over the beauty of the great English ballerina, Margot Fonteyn.

Here is the two-part report I wrote on that revealing encounter, with expletives now undeleted:

☆ ☆ ☆

Newport Beach — a sprawling, sun-basking suburb of the Los Angeles megalopolis with high-rise motels and rows of condominium cliff dwellings shining on its hills, rank after rank of shopping centers and parking lots marching the length of its arroyos, and yachts like sparkling rings on the fingers of its bay — counts as its most famous citizen 68-year-old film star John Wayne.

I have just returned from an extraordinary encounter, in the company of 40 other newspaper people, with Wayne inside the compound of his beautiful bay-front home, to which he invited us for cocktails just before seeing a special screening of his latest film, "Brannigan," a detective melodrama produced by his son Michael, who also directed.

With the grinning truculence he has so long reflected on the screen, Wayne attacked the press, defended his politics and, near the end of the evening, cried out for the kind of beauty represented by retired English prima ballerina Margot Fonteyn.

It was such an unusual and oddly endearing — if slightly boozey — performance that I have decided to report it. I happened to have my tape recorder along and got Wayne's O.K. to use it while my associates frantically took notes on paper napkins from the bar. I propose to counterpoint my tape of the evening's discourse with his remarks on many of the same subjects during the official, somewhat more formal, and contrastingly sober press conference the next morning.

Party conversation — "The Night Before" — is set in bold-face type, and press conference questions and answers — "The Morning After" — in regular light-face type.

As further preamble, I should make it clear that we party guests had the same access to alcoholic refreshments that our host did, although not all of us could match the 6-4, 263-pound Wayne's thirst — or capacity.

The scene "TNB" was the front lawn, running down to the water, then the terrace, and finally the den of Wayne's home. The scene "TMA" was a meeting-room at the Newporter Inn, with Wayne on a dais and the rest of us in chairs, classroom style.

The Night Before:

WAYNE: You know, I have the reputation of being an extreme right-winger. I just don't go for what is called a liberal today. But I thought of myself as a liberal for years.

QUESTION (Howard): When John Dos Passos died it was pointed out that as a young man he had been liberal to the point of radicalism, but as an old man he was considered very, very conservative. Don't you think it may be the times that change?

W.: They haven't changed me a goddamned bit!

Q.: You mean you think today that you're still liberal?

W.: I know I am. I listen to everybody's point of view. I listen to everybody.

Q.: In view of your support for Richard Nixon, how can you consider yourself a liberal, though?

W.: Are you under the impression that President Nixon was a conservative? I mean, your political background is a little shortsighted! Pardon me, I'm going to have another drink. You can't believe that Nixon was a conservative!

The Morning After:
    Q.: You sounded disillusioned with politics last night.
    W.: I am. That ought to be pretty plain. I am.
    Q.: Does that mean you won't do any more campaigning?
    W.: I can't say that. The only time I've ever spoken up was when I thought that I should. I have never been interested in politics and I've liked very few politicians, but those that I've liked I've gone to bat for. Some for good, and some for bad.

The Night Before:
    Q.: What do you think about the cut-off of aid to Cambodia?
    W.: I can't give you a sermon on the mount about that. But of course I think it's stupid. I was over there. I know that — look how the goddamned horrible bastards are killing those people now, where they don't need to. That's not our people. That's their people that are doing it. They needed our help. We gave it to them until LBJ got a little scared and backed off — sneaked a lot of men in there and then let a lot of politicians tell him what to do instead of either winning the goddamned war or leaving. And he put us on the spot. But he was a hell of a nice guy. He just made a mistake, that's all. I mean, guys make mistakes. The only

terrible thing is that a lot of people in your business, looking for provocative stories because you're on television now and selling Toyotas and trucks and all that crap — you look for provocative stories rather than be decent and honorable and thoughtful about our country, and it bothers me. The hell with it. It's none of my damn business. I'm not in your racket. Please do not nece-goddam-ssarily quote me.

The Morning After:

> Q.: You made some remarks last night.
>
> W.: I probably did.
>
> Q.: Do you remember any of them?
>
> W.: Well, you know the dentist had been hammering on my jaw yesterday afternoon, and it was full of Novocain. And then they give you that codeine and aspirin — and the whisky and the tequila — so I was pretty rough on you, I guess. But that's my wont. Anything about Cambodia, ask my producers. I want to stop this hearsay. What you hear from our producer back there, Mr. Jules Levy, comes to you direct. He's the expert on it. Jules will now get up and answer questions on Cambodia — all questions on Cambodia.
>
> (Only of course he didn't. One surmises that Levy may have criticized Wayne's outspokenness on the subject The Night Before.)

The Night Before:

> **QUESTION (Howard): How would you define a liberal? I have a definition that I think. . .**
>
> **WAYNE: Are you going to define it or do you want to**

hear mine? My semantics of a liberal is a man who will listen to and deliberate over another man's point of view.

Q.: And is willing to change his mind? That's mine, too.

W.: Right! But these modern so-called liberals not only won't change their minds, they won't even listen to you.

The Morning After:

W.: I had never considered myself a conservative, but some fellows who write in these newspapers and on TV say that I'm a right-wing extremist, so I guess I am. The first fellow I proselyted for was the most liberal governor we ever had in California — a Democrat named Culbert Olsen. Gordon McLendon is a Democrat from Texas that I went for. Then I went for Barry Goldwater and Nixon, and my "fellow artist," Reagan. Those are the men that I've gone for. They're a mixture of all kinds of backgrounds.

The Night Before:

Q.: **What do you think of Nixon and Agnew these days?**

W.: I loved Agnew. I enjoyed Agnew. Down here we have wonderful people. Agnew came down and spoke to us, and we had a great deal of feeling for the man. I guess he did something wrong. (Laughter) No, now — none of that half-assed laughter. I'm not sure he did anything terribly wrong. But in order to get out of the way because there might be some Administration trouble, he said, "I'll accept this." So I don't know what the hell he did or didn't do. All I know is he was a delightful man. . . .

Q.: Have you spoken to Mr. Nixon since he resigned?
W.: Yes.

(United Artists publicist: "The buses are here!" They weren't, but he stopped the flow. Wayne said he'd talk about Nixon "in the morning.")

The Morning After:

Q.: You mentioned last night and didn't get to finish your answer, that you had met or talked to Mr. Nixon. Can you tell us about it, please?

W.: Talked to Nixon? I've talked to him lots of times.

Q.: Yes, but since his resignation?

W.: Oh, just to say hello. I've never sat down and gone over his retrospect with him. I don't know what he's. . .

Q.: Did you talk to him on the telephone?

W.: Yes. Certainly.

The Night Before:

W.: I don't want to get mixed up in politics. I've found that my kind of thinking. . . A bunch of your so-called goddamned liberals. . . No, I'm tired of all that stuff. The kind of thing that I like is this. (He picks up a large book about Dame Margot Fonteyn, the British ballerina, from his coffee table.) Can I show you some of the most beautiful things that I have ever seen in my whole life? Why have you put me on this spot? Let's look at real beauty. Oh God! She's the most beautiful person that I know in my whole life. Whoever did this book captured this woman in this thing. (He opens the book and reads): "March 28, 1970, Stuttgart, Germany. Dear Miss Fonteyn: If the way you do everything could be summed up in one word, that word would be the most beautiful word in the world. . . ."

Now can you imagine anything more delightful than that? And look at her axis. Isn't that magnificent? And so you ask me about President this and President that. It's things like this (still holding the book open) that are important — the beauty of our wonderful world! If you'd just think about that instead of everybody trying to think about nasty things. What's happened to decency and honor?

The Morning After:

Q.: Mr. Wayne, we've talked about your views on Watergate and Cambodia and other things. I wonder if you would mind talking a bit about yourself and your life these days. Your life has probably changed in the last few years — friends dying. I have read that you are often depressed. Can you tell us about these things?

W.: True, true. I try to make some more friends before they all die off. I don't remember all those depressions. But I feel a tremendous loss in Jack (John) Ford and Ward Bond. They were lifelong friends, and I spent so many hours of so many days with them that naturally there's a vacancy. But I changed my life style two or three times. I don't live out in the Valley any more, I live here at the beach. I have yachting friends, tennis friends. I try not to get caught in a little group where it really hurts when you lose one. When we lost Harry Carey, that was a big blow to my life. I loved Harry. Sometimes when I was a younger man, it was a shock to find out that people died. But now I know they do.

☆ ☆ ☆

Both the party and the press conference went on at far greater length than I have had space to reproduce. But I hope I have fairly represented John Wayne at both, with the contrasting moods the two events invited.

I interviewed Wayne several times on film locations and at premieres, but this was the only time I ever saw him drop his guard and reveal himself so fully. I liked him immensely.

I found him both a brighter and a subtler man than I had assumed — a man who loved life and filmmaking. He was also a man who loved his country. That his ideas about what was best for it may have differed from mine seemed to me no reason to belittle him. He was a man of strong beliefs and passions, and he spoke out for both.

I was sorry he resented the press so much, but readily admit that he had some cause, if not, perhaps, as much as he thought. He had so much vitality and good humor, even when he was angry about something, that you wished you could get him on your side.

But we should remember that he never claimed to be anything but a working actor. Amazingly today, more than 20 years after his 1979 death, surveys show that he is still — on the strength of his endlessly re-run films on the cable movie channels — our most popular male movie star.

Duke? He's still the king.

Chapter 5

LUCILLE BALL: ONE LEGEND WHO LOVED IT

If John Wayne was the Grand Canyon of film stars, Lucille Ball was perhaps the Niagara Falls, bright and shimmering and ceaselessly bubbling and flowing. To change the figure of speech, the two of them had become, towards the end of their careers, Mr. and Mrs. America, as Ball herself observed to me after their appearance together on a TV special.

The observation came in the course of an interview I did with her on the set of "Mame," the musical, in Hollywood in 1973. Before it was over, I was drawn into a dialogue with her that had me as confused, and amused, as Ricky Ricardo in a "Lucy" episode. By the time we were through, I was practically slapping my forehead and spouting Spanish.

☆ ☆ ☆

Let me set the scene: We were on Stage 9 at the old Columbia Pictures lot in the heart of Hollywood. It was just a rental lot, Columbia having moved in with Warner Bros. in Burbank at what had become The Burbank Studio. Warner Bros.' "Mame" company, which had been scheduled to film Burnside Plantation scenes at the Disney Ranch that day, had been forced inside by rain, and they had hastily set up the courtroom scene in the closest available studio space.

While director Gene Saks, choreographer Onna White, and all their myriad assistants and crews rehearsed the extras to a playback of the "Open a New Window" number, Lucille Ball, sweltering in a white fox-collared, full-length ermine coat, more or less relaxed against a reclining board, designed to take as much weight off a star's feet as possible while wrinkling her costume as little as possible. Intermittently, she cooled herself with a Japanese fan, and periodically she marched onto the set to rehearse and do short takes of the scene. In between times, she talked to me — cordially, thoughtfully, wittily, and always interestedly.

I told her my favorite Lucille Ball film — pre-TV — was a 1949 comedy with William Holden called "Miss Grant Takes Richmond," and suggested that it seemed to contain the seeds of her first TV character, Lucy Ricardo.

"I'm glad you liked it," she smiled, her huge violet eyes widening even more. "And you're right. When I made up my mind to go into television, that was the film I chose as a kind of model. I had to sit down and really dissect what I had done. There had been 30 or 40 pictures, and I thought, now what do I like in any of them? I looked for the sweet moments, you know — not mushy, but nice moments. There were one or two in some of the other pictures, but in that one there were many. And when I put them all together in my mind, they were nearly all domestic situations — sweet, lovable, gentle moments, with just enough zaniness.

"Bill was so good at comedy, but those long locations far away have been his wont for many years, and for many reasons. I wanted him to do another comedy with me a few years ago, but he said, 'Lucy, I'd love to do another comedy with you, but I'm looking for those epics where I go and stay.'"

I asked her if she had always been a natural clown.

"Oh, there was always a little spontaneous combustion. When I was younger, I wasn't very attractive, so in school I wanted to be a cheerleader, which I was. Just active physically, I think, was the way I was. I didn't do terribly daring things. I had the first boy bob, the first open galoshes, the first swinging opossum coat, and the first red cloche hat, like they're wearing in this film."

Did she intend to do comedy from the start in films?

"I never thought of anything else because I started as a showgirl. When I left the showgirl era at Goldwyn, I came to Columbia and worked in short-reel comedies with the Three Stooges. Boy, that was a training ground. You learned to take seltzer in the face and go home soaked every night. I didn't regret it, but I sure didn't like it. That wasn't my idea of something to do, but I never complained.

"When we lost our job after three months I was kind of glad, because it looked like short-reel comedies were gonna be it for me over here (at Columbia). I was out of work for two hours, then went down the street to RKO and stayed there for seven years."

When she came back from doing a scene, I said, "Speaking of cheerleaders, you're still one. You were really trying to pep up the extras."

"You bet," she grinned. "People like this have a tendency not to pay much attention to what they're doing till it's time to eat. The longer they take to get a scene right, the more money it is in their pockets. They have a kind of ennui that's ingrained." (I learned later that Ball had invested heavily in the film.)

My next question led us into what sounded more and more like one of Lucy's comedy routines, proving she didn't need her writers to be funny. All I said was, "Was there ever a time when you suddenly woke up and realized that you were a legend and practically an institution?"

"Well," she began, "I had read things like that and heard them repeated many times, but I don't think it had ever sunk in until I read John Wayne's and my. . . obituary is what it was, in an editorial following that patriotic TV special of his in which I appeared as the Statue of Liberty.

"It was a rave about us, but it was an obituary. It was like the last words ever to be written about us, and we were coupled in it, as if we were somehow Mr. and Mrs. America. Of course, it didn't say there was nowhere else for us to go, but it was like we had already gone. I don't think he was as aware of the finality of it as I was. He looked on it as a grand write-up about us, but I said, 'John! It was an obituary, and I just want to tell you how happy I am to be buried alongside you.'

"I think that's the first time I went, 'Oooh,' and realized there might be something to that 'living legend' bit. Of course, I've had a few — what do you call 'em? — testimonial dinners that are a little nerve-wracking, where the entire town is there to pay you tribute, and you think, they could have waited, you know, a couple of years more. It's like they think I might not make it or something."

Howard: "You don't mind being considered a legend, then?"

Lucy: "How could you mind that?"

H.: "Some say they do."

Lucy: "Really? Legends tell you that? Alleged legends, or people who have never become living legends have said that?"

H.: "People have been quoted as saying that."

Lucy: "I don't know what the hell you answered me. I'm not sure I know what I asked you. What did you say?"

H.: "I said, do you mind being a living legend?"

Lucy: "No. And you said other people have minded, and I said. . . ."

H.: "I said other people have been quoted as minding."

Lucy: "Were those already living legends, or were they only living — the ones that minded?"

H.: "They were considered living legends."

Lucy: "And they minded it?" . . . You mean, like Bette Davis?"

H.: "She was one, as a matter of fact."

Lucy: "Did she mind it?"

H.: "Yes, she was quoted as saying she didn't believe in all that rubbish."

Lucy: "I'll go along with what. But I don't know what she means. There are different ways to not believe.

"Do you know what I mean by that? I don't. But what

is it she doesn't believe? Helen Hayes has had to live with the 'first lady of the American theatre' legend, and she denies it vehemently. She goes to great lengths. . . but there's nothing that can stop her from being 'the first lady of the American theatre.' She is, you know.

"That doesn't make ALL of us living legends, but there are certain terms, I realize as you stretch into longevity in the industry, that they apply to you. It's like farewell appearances. You didn't mean it to be your farewell appearance, but after they said it again and again — so much that it sounded like farewell — you kinda hesitated to go out for a few months. You're not ungrateful at all, but you think THEY must be tired of it. What is there left to say?"

H.: "Do you have any plans for a farewell appearance, or maybe a series of them like Jack Benny?"

Lucy: "No! They're foisted upon you. I don't ever plan to retire."

There were other questions and other stories — like how she broke her leg a year before while standing perfectly still on a Colorado ski slope. ("This old broad slid by and screwed me into the ground; now I've got three screws in my leg and I'll never ski again — but I'll ski-tour.") But I had to stop somewhere. Stop, and simply say that at 62 and with three screws in one leg, Lucille Ball still had a great pair of legs, a firm chin line, the biggest eyes this side of Sophia Loren, and one of the sharpest wits and the best heads in show business.

☆ ☆ ☆

Just over a year later, I got to talk with Ball again at the world premiere of "Mame," a glittering affair held in Atlanta and outside the city at Sen. Herman Talmadge's Talmadge Farms, some twenty miles north of Atlanta. It was a Beauregard Burnside-style hunt breakfast celebrating the arrival of the film musical, starring Lucille Ball and Robert Preston.

The white-columned house was "one of only two in the ay-ree-ah that Shuhman missed," smiling Sen. Talmadge told me as we stood near the groaning breakfast board, laden with country ham, hot biscuits, country sausage, scrambled egg casserole, cheese grits, strawberries, individual pecan pies, and coffee.

While the Senator strolled amiably through his crowded house before finally settling solitarily with a cigar into a front porch rocker, Lady Bird Johnson chatted in low tones in a corner of the diningroom with her late husband's secretary of state, Dean Rusk, about the importance of the selection of a new dean for the University of Pennsylvania. Mrs. Johnson's connection with "Mame" was that the benefit premiere showing the night before in Atlanta had been to help raise funds for the Lyndon B. Johnson Memorial Grove in Lady Bird Johnson Park on the Potomac, just across the river from Washington.

But we of the press and television were not there merely to sip mint juleps and eat country ham and grits, and stare at the celebrities; we were there primarily to interview the main honoree of the day, Mame herself, Miss Lucille Ball.

Although I had interviewed Ball on the "Mame" set in Hollywood just a little over a year before, there was a question I hadn't asked then and wanted to ask now after seeing the finished film.

"Miss Ball," I said, "you do a kind of comedy which it

seems to me most women are not able to do. You and Carole Lombard and Kay Kendall in their day always managed to be funny without losing your dignity or your femininity.

"Most female comics, it seems to me, lose both. Is there a secret that you have?"

Said the delightful lady: "I don't know how to answer that. I never do. But if there is a secret, maybe it's this: I just believe in any unbelievable situation I'm given, and I don't do a lot of mugging, which some of the girls did, and do. Some of them aren't around anymore. I've even forgotten their names. You know who I mean, but I can't think of their names. . . ."

"Martha Raye, Cass Daley. . . ," I volunteered.

"Yeah, Cass, Martha. They mugged a lot. But I've never done that. Carole and Kay never did that. We did comedic situations.

". . . just as slapstick as the others, but you. . ."

"Yeah. Well, Vivian (Vance) and I never had to mug. We just talked and did, and I think we acted more in the . . . What do you call 'em, the fat one and the thin one?

"Laurel and Hardy?"

"Yeah, we used the Laurel and Hardy technique. The more ridiculous the situation, the more we believed it and the more seriously we took it."

Someone asked how Ball managed to get through the energetic dances in "Mame" with her recently broken leg, cracked in three places in a skiing accident.

"I managed it because of the amazing preparation of a young woman named Onna White, a very unusual young woman who choreographed the picture. I don't know if you know her work or not."

"Yes," I affirmed. "The way she used the camera in 'Mame' was incredible. She choreographed the camera as well as the dances."

Ball fixed me with an almost accusing stare.

"How do you know that?" she demanded. "Do you know that much about pictures?"

"Well," I said, "I saw the film, and you can see it on the screen, what she did."

"A lot of people can't," the actress insisted. "The cutter, Maury Winetrobe, is a great editor, one of the really great ones. He said that the stuff Onna shot he just pasted together and it fit perfectly. He didn't have anything to do on the dance numbers. She had conceived it all in her head and shot it exactly the way it was supposed to end up.

"When we were shooting, Onna would start us and we'd go 'Dah-Dee-Dah-Dah. . .' and she'd say, 'Cut!' And we'd be left like this (she freezes, arms extended), and I'd say, 'What's wrong?,' and she'd say, 'Nothing. That's all I needed.' She's fantastic."

Ball does her own singing — she's got a beautiful baritone voice without much music in it but a lot of feeling — and one of our group complimented her on it. She fixed the lady with a self-belittling stare:

"I can't sing and you know it! But thank you, darling. They insisted I do the songs myself, so I said, well, I'll just do the best I can because I believe in them so much. So I recorded them. But I am a little embarrassed because, after all, we can't all be Eydie Gorme, and I wish I could be. But let's not talk about that.

"I got through it, and if you accept it, I appreciate it."

☆ ☆ ☆

"Mame" proved to be a disappointment, both artistically and commercially, although Ball gave it her best shot. Having invested some money in it, she went on the road to promote it, but it failed, anyway. Nobody was really anti-"Mame," but instead of going out to see her as Auntie Mame, most people were content to sit at home and watch her younger self as Lucy Ricardo in "I Love Lucy" re-runs.

Though she lived another 15 years, and continued to work in television, she never made another theatrical motion picture. When she appeared with Bob Hope on the Academy Awards show on March 29, 1989, he thought she seemed terribly tired. Her hand felt weak as he clasped it, and he called the next day to see how she was feeling. Less than a month later she was dead. Her heart, big as it was, had simply given out.

Chapter 6

WHERE THERE'S LIFE, THERE'S BOB HOPE

They say hope springs eternal, and Bob Hope seems to BE eternal. The man who stood holding Lucille Ball's hand in her last public appearance — on the 1989 Oscarcast, less than a month before she died — was 56 years old when I interviewed him some 40 years ago about whether he might be retiring soon.

I had first met Hope in 1948 when a young blond singer named Doris Day was still touring with him, along with Les Brown's Band of Renown. Eleven years later, when Hope arrived in Memphis in May, 1959, for his personal appearance at the Memphis Cotton Carnival, I met him at the airport after midnight and rode in to Hotel Peabody with him in his limousine, conducting a catch-as-catch-can interview while he used me as an audience for what was probably a warm-up of his

Cotton Carnival routine.

A week or so earlier, the newspapers had been filled with reports that Hope had suffered a blood clot in one eye, and there was speculation that he might be retiring soon. But sitting there in the limo with him I thought, if Bob Hope is sick, I must be dead.

Let's say, for the sake of argument, that the blood clot in his eye had throttled him down to half speed. Even as a half-wit he was twice as funny as any other comedian I've ever interviewed, with the possible exception of Peter Sellers.

Hope arrived from Los Angeles after midnight for his Cotton Carnival personal appearance. He stepped down the ramp with that familiar, whimsical swagger, his eyes glancing about as if he expected to be arrested.

From the moment he got off, he was "on."

In fact, I suspect that one of the reasons Hope's doctors had ordered him to slow down was that he was always "on" — whether the audience was one person, 5,000, or 30 million on television.

Even on the drive to the hotel, when he could have sat back and relaxed and answered my questions straight, the inveterate golfer kept swinging.

Retire?

"I'm never going to retire!," he crackled. "I've got a few jokes I'm saving for on the way to the last hole. Sure I'm gonna take it a little easy. This eye isn't going to get any better until I do.

"But all this business about the end of the road and retiring — I don't go for that! Life magazine wanted to shoot a layout of me in action on this trip and then do another of me

The author looks on as Bob Hope is welcomed to a theatre owners'
convention in Memphis in 1959. (Photo courtesy of William Speer)

relaxing in Florida with my wife and kids, like that's what I'll be
doing from now on.

"I don't go for that baloney!"

Hope said he had finished his last television show for
the season. He was through for the summer except for two
weeks at Cain Park in Cleveland Heights, Ohio.

"One show a night," he said, "and that'll be fun because
it's my hometown."

"What about another movie?," I wondered. "Alias Jesse
James" was getting rave reviews. "Even Time magazine," I
pointed out, "liked this one."

"Yeah," said Hope with a grin. "Those guys must be
drinkin'. If The New Yorker ever likes me, I'll just quit. That
John McCarten — instead of a piece of paper, he puts a fang in

the typewriter! He's the guy who knocked the San Francisco earthquake — said it didn't have heart.

"But the critic I like was a guy back home in Cleveland. I went back there for a show and he said, 'Here's a man who came up from nothing — and brought it back with him.'"

Just then we passed a bus. Hope ducked down to get a better view out the window. "What was that?," he demanded with a snicker. "Elvis Presley's town car?"

Speaking of Elvis, Hope said: "When I went to Germany last winter, I thought it would be nice to get Elvis to do a show with me. He was already over there. I got the Army's O.K. Gen. Maxwell Taylor said it would be all right.

"But I guess Elvis's Colonel Parker out-ranked him. He thought I was trying to steal Elvis for the Army's Special Services or something. I said I just wanted to do one show with him, but nothing ever came of it. We kept going round and round and I finally gave up."

Hope reiterated that he wasn't ready to give up his career quite yet, though. Despite his bad eye, he squinted into the future and still saw plenty of Hope.

☆ ☆ ☆

How right he was. He's lived so long the Cold War ended and most of the boys he entertained overseas at Christmas time came home. But at 99, there was still life, and there was still Hope.

Chapter 7

Michael Caine & Sean Connery: Two Sirs, With Love

Few would have predicted when Thomas Connery was born in 1930 in Edinburgh, Scotland, to an Irish tinker and his charlady wife that 70 years later he would kneel before his Queen to be knighted for his accomplishments and good works. And who would have thought that another future knight was born in 1933 in the charity wing of St. Olave's Hospital in South London to the Micklewhites — a fish market porter and his wife, also a charlady who cleaned other people's houses?

These two young men would not meet for almost 20 years, but their lives were already on parallel courses. Connery, looking older than his 15 years, quit school and joined the Royal Navy in 1945 just as World War II was ending. Maurice "Mick" Micklewhite had to quit school and go to work at 13. At age 18, he was conscripted into the National Service and the

Royal Fusiliers just in time for the Korean War of 1950-53, serving first on occupation duty in Germany, and then in combat in Korea.

After being mustered out of the services, the two young men followed different routes toward the same goal — careers in the theatre, television and films, each earning his first screen credits in 1956. But by this time, they had been casual acquaintances for five years, having met in 1951 at one of the then popular "bottle parties" (what Americans used to call "BYOB," or Bring Your Own Bottle parties) enjoyed by bit and supporting players in London's West End after final curtains had fallen. Caine was appearing in a play while Connery was a member of the sailor's chorus in "South Pacific."

By 1956, Connery had exchanged his Thomas for the more euphonius Sean. Although born Irish, his father was a confirmed Scot, and Scottish independence was to become, along with education, one of the son's favorite causes.

Young Micklewhite was by now on his second name change. After re-naming himself Michael Scott, he was informed when he applied for Equity membership that the actors' union already had a Michael Scott. His agent, about to ink a contract for him, told him he had to come up with another new name within the hour. Walking through Leicester Square as he wracked his brain for another name, he looked up at a theatre marquee and saw the name of Humphrey Bogart, an actor he idolized. Bogey was starring in a new film called "The Caine Mutiny." That was it! He would become Michael Caine.

As the '60s rolled around, the Cold War began heating up, and the British were sending their spies over, under and around the Iron Curtain that now separated Communist Eastern Europe and the Soviet Union from the West. As in real life, so in the movies and, as fate, or luck, would have it, both Connery and Caine were about to achieve major stardom as British spies in this new wave of action entertainment.

Connery clicked first as the suave and sexy Agent 007 in the inaugural film of Ian Fleming's James Bond series, "Dr. No," in 1962. Then in 1965, Caine's career took off when he played novelist Len Deighton's buttoned-down, horn-rimmed spy, Harry Palmer, in "The Ipcress File."

Caine played Palmer in two more films, "Funeral in Berlin" and "Billion-Dollar Brain," but was able to vary his roles with successful outings in such films as "Alfie," which won him an Oscar nomination, "The Wrong Box," and "Woman Times Seven." Connery, in contrast, was finding himself typed as 007, the spy with the license to kill. The role was beginning to kill him, and, he feared, his career, and, after six films he finally escaped his Bondage following the release of "Diamonds Are Forever" in 1971.

By the time I had an opportunity to interview Connery in February of 1979 in New Orleans, however, he was at another crossroad in his career. He had let it be known that he was now interested in re-assuming the mantle of Ian Fleming's famous intelligence operative, and I couldn't resist asking why.

"Why not," the big, balding 48-year-old Scotsman challenged me. I may have flinched ever so slightly before his seeming wrath turned into a softer, and more expansive, answer.

"I first got involved," he said, "in what was simply a project of rewriting with Len Deighton a Bond story we're calling, very originally, 'James Bond of the Secret Service.'"

(A little cross-fertilization there, with Deighton working on a Fleming story.)

"It started out really as just that — a writing exercise with a friend. Then I reached the stage where I considered doing it myself — playing the role again — and I just got in under the wire on the project.

"Now, however, there's a big debate and legal wrangle between two different studios that are involved in the project. It had nothing to do with me, and I really can't say any more about the dispute than that. It is in negotiation, and we hope to be able to get it under way soon."

But why, I persisted, after being so eager to get away from the character he had created in "Dr. No," and refined and developed in "From Russia With Love," "Goldfinger," "Thunderball," "You Only Live Twice," and "Diamonds Are Forever," was Connery now willing, even eager, to play 007 again?

"I'm not the same person I was when I played it before," he said. "When I left the part, it was because I wanted to go ahead and do other things that would be rewarding to me — different types of films, different types of parts. Having done that, it doesn't seem such a drastic step for me to go back and do a Bond film."

Connery had indeed established his considerable range as an actor in such varied films as Sidney Lumet's "The Hill," as a radical poet opposite Joanne Woodward in "A Fine Madness," and as the ruminant, middle-aged Robin Hood opposite the haunting presence of Audrey Hepburn's Maid Marian in Richard Lester's evocative "Robin and Marian." But wasn't there a danger, I suggested, that in returning to the

Bond role, he might become typed again as the cool, sardonic, resourceful stud?

"I don't think it works that way at all," he said. "The amount of work you've done in any field shows. Now that I've done a variety of roles in a variety of pictures, I think that versatility will reveal itself in anything I do. It is imprinted on the public consciousness. After all, in films, the good things and the bad things you've done stay with you. Films, unlike stage performances, are always there for posterity."

It took almost four years to iron out the legal problems connected with the project, but Connery finally did play Bond again in a 1983 re-make of "Thunderball" appropriately entitled "Never Say Never Again."

Connery had come to New Orleans for the Southern premiere of writer-director Michael Crichton's "The Great Train Robbery." Based on Crichton's novel of several years earlier, it was not a re-make of the 11-minute 1903 Western usually recognized as the first story film, but the true story of a mid-19th century train robbery in Great Britain.

The big news at the premiere was that Connery, as the mastermind of the robbery, had done his own stunts.

"It wasn't my original intention to do the stunts," he told me in his beguiling Scottish brogue. "It just became apparent as we rehearsed the train sequences in Ireland that if we wanted to make them really work, I was going to have to do them."

A weight-lifter and Mr. Universe contestant in his youth, the 48-year-old Scot still had the stamina to climb out of a first-class railway carriage, walk the tops of four cars on a speeding train back to the baggage car, lower himself by ropes to the locked doors, unlock them, effect the robbery, climb back up to the top of the train with his loot, and make his way back to his carriage. A series of low overpasses kept him ducking. Strong winds nearly blew him off the train, and did cause a dangerous, unplanned spill.

"I don't know what the insurance risks were," Connery continued, " — terrific, I imagine — but the director (author Crichton) was eager for me to attempt the stunts, and there was no restraining order from the producer. If I hadn't done the whole thing myself, we would have had to photograph it in such a way that the audience, in watching the film, would have said, 'Ah, we're going to the double now.'"

His physical stamina has undoubtedly been one of the reasons for Connery's long career, and he was aware of its importance that day in New Orleans when he was a mere 48 years old, and a decade away from becoming Harrison Ford's father, for gosh sakes, in 1989's "Indiana Jones and the Last Crusade."

"I think you've got to have the stamina of a rugby player to sustain a long film career," he said. And his is still going after almost half a century.

Although to Americans, Connery's Bond seemed prototypically English, he said that initially, he had a difficult time being accepted as English in England. "I don't know," he grinned, "I guess I was too Polish-looking or something."

He has always made the distinction off-screen that he is Scottish rather than English. And, although over the years he has maintained homes in Malaga, Spain, and Monte Carlo, he has always remained devoted to his Scottish homeland. He has given generously over the years to the Scottish International

Education Trust, including his million-dollar salary for "Diamonds Are Forever." He has also been deeply involved with the Scottish Nationalist Party, with the goal of independence for Scotland.

"In fact," he confided, "I'm totally in favor of ALL fragmentation. The sooner you break up the United States, the better. The smaller the pieces, the more chances there are for everybody."

Our 50 states are still united, more or less, but Connery could feel a measure of satisfaction when Scotland, though still a part of the United Kingdom, finally achieved its own parliament in 1999, 292 years after it had united its parliament with England's. A year later Queen Elizabeth II knighted him in Edinburgh in what must have seemed a profound culmination as well as the beginning of a new century for Sir Thomas (Sean) Connery.

☆ ☆ ☆

Connery and Caine co-starred for the first time in 1975 in one of the best films either of them ever made. It was director and co-scenarist John Huston's brilliant adaptation of Rudyard Kipling's "The Man Who Would Be King," in which a pair of British soldier-buddies decide to resign from the army and set up their own little kingdom in Kafiristan, benignly accepting tributes of gold and jewels from the warlike Kafirs.

Five years before "The Man Who Would Be King," I had learned a great deal about Michael Caine's own real-life war experiences, his feelings about war in general, and some of his strong opinions on a variety of other subjects.

Let me set the scene for you: We are in the Medill Room of the Bismarck Hotel in Chicago in the spring of 1970. A dozen of us newspaper types have just seen a screening of an intriguing and unconventional war film called "Too Late the Hero," co-starring Caine with Henry Fonda, Cliff Robertson and Denholm Elliott.

Caine arrives for the small press cocktail and dinner party with a reputation for assertiveness and even rebellion against convention and class barriers, not unlike his Cockney character in "Alfie" a few years before. (Just how closely the actor identified with that character would be confirmed some years later when he wrote his autobiography and entitled it "What's It All About?")

With cocktails, the verbal sparring begins, particularly with a couple of film critics who claim modestly to be World War II infantry veterans and feel defensive about "their" war.

They suggest that "Too Late the Hero," which chronicles British-vs.-Japanese patrol action in the New Hebrides Islands in 1942, is anti-war and an attack on WWII in particular. I suggest rather that it is an attack on conventional ideas of combat heroism.

Caine picks up on that and points out that everybody is against war. "Even Hitler," he suggests, "would rather have taken over Europe without having to fight."

The two critics begin their questions with "as a former infantryman," but one says later, "Actually, I was an Air Force type," and the other eventually admits that he was an infantry officer who never saw combat, but "loved the infantry." (As one who spent a year and a half in the infantry in Italy in 1944-45,

I never knew an infantryman who loved the infantry.)

Out of this verbal friction between 6:30 and 10 p.m. emerges the following portrait of Michael Caine as he was in the spring of 1970, painted in his own words, gestures and facial expressions. In the background of the portrait are student demonstrations against President Richard Nixon and the Vietnam War, which will continue until a cease-fire is signed in Paris almost three years later. Having himself spent a year in infantry combat in Korea, Caine has strong feelings about war and heroism.

"I made this film," he declares, "as a kind of antidote to 'The Green Berets' (superhawk John Wayne's 1968 cinematic statement of support for the Vietnam War), which advocated a kind of heroism I don't believe exists and a commitment in Vietnam which I think is foolish and tragic.

"My basic view — and I think this is what our film says — is that nobody goes into battle screaming they're going to kill those dirty Viet Cong, or whoever, for God and country. I think you are simply manipulated into a position where if you don't kill the enemy, he is going to kill you, and that what we've called heroism is simply self-preservation, or a bond that has developed between you and a buddy so that you try to save him. I think young men faced with going into battle ought to know that — and their mothers and fathers ought to know that.

"There are just wars and unjust wars. World War II and Korea were just wars — and if an invader lands at the White Cliffs of Dover, I'm prepared to die tomorrow. But why lose your young men in Vietnam and Cambodia? America has never done anything with malevolence in its heart. It went into Vietnam with the best motives in the world. Incidentally, how many students marching against the Vietnam War know it was their hero John F. Kennedy who sent the first combat troops in? But you should get out now and stop killing American boys.

"Basically, I think the students are right about racism, Vietnam, Cambodia, and Nixon. But I also remember that before World War II, students supported Neville Chamberlain with banners saying, 'Kill the Warmonger, Winston Churchill.' And so I am not prepared to live in a country run by 18-year-olds not out of school yet.

"The United States is the most self-critical country I've ever known. You're not perfect, but what country is? Look at Britain — how fouled up we are. But why should you fear Russia so much? They're just trying to get what you've got, and when they've got it, they won't be Communist anymore. They say 'Down with the bourgeoisie,' but their aim is simply to give everybody a house, a refrigerator and a car. Once they've got them, they'll all be the bourgeoisie they used to say 'Down with!' China is already saying Russia is too bourgeois.

"I'm not much for politics. I am not a member of any political party, but I pay England's socialist taxes. I come from the lower class — I mean, I'm not asking for your sympathy, because that would be silly, wouldn't it? But now I'm a 37-year-old Limey actor who rides around in a Rolls-Royce. And when I drive around England and look out the window of that Rolls-Royce, I see no beggars, no sick, no poor, and so I can look out that window with no guilt, no bad conscience. I don't know if I'm a socialist, but I am a humanist. I believe people have the right NOT to die of starvation, or of exposure, or of untreated illnesses — and they can't die of those things in England today. I promise you they can't do it — it's against the law. And I believe in that"

In June of the year 2000, one month before similar ceremonies for Connery in Edinburgh, the Queen knighted Maurice Micklewhite at Buckingham Palace, dubbing him Sir Michael Caine, a name he had certainly earned.

☆ ☆ ☆

Now, how to sum up the careers of these two "parfit, gentil" acting knights, who rose from low birth to high accomplishments and honors? Perhaps I should simply paraphrase Leigh Hunt's poem, "The Gentle Armour," and say:

"There lived two knights, long after knighthood was in flow'r,/ Who charmed alike the tilt-yard and the bower."

Chapter 8

ELVIS: FROM THE BEGINNING TO THE END

I can still see him as he looked on July 27, 1954, when he walked into my Memphis Press-Scimitar office on the fifth floor of what had once been a Ford assembly plant. Except for the pre-tied bow-tie nestling just below his adam's apple, he looked like he might be an assembly line worker himself. His shirt and pants and gray leisure jacket didn't quite go together. His plastered-down, growing-out, flat-top haircut with duck-tail looked as if it had been administered by a lawn mower. His pimply face and long, scraggly sideburns stirred not a ripple among the women in the office. And yet there was something about him. You could imagine young girls being intrigued by his slumbrous eyes and curly, almost surly, mouth.

Elvis Presley was first recorded a block from my office and, as most of the Elvis books will tell you, the first interview he ever gave was for my Press-Scimitar column, The Front Row, on July 28, 1954. By the spring of 1957, when I was at Paramount, asking people like Sophia Loren, Lizabeth Scott and Doris Day what they thought of him, he had already taken the country by storm.

From one-nighters across the South, he had wiggled his way to New York and appearances on the Ed Sullivan and Steve Allen shows, to his first engagement in Las Vegas, and to Hollywood to star in "Love Me Tender," the just-completed "Loving You" at Paramount, and "Jailhouse Rock," which was just going into production at MGM.

Three years earlier, on the eve of his first record release, my interview with the 19-year-old had taken only about 15 or 20 minutes. Afterwards, I took him back to our photo studio, and the photographer on duty snapped a single picture of him — a head shot which ran with my column the next day.

To tell you the truth, the interview was more with my old friend, the late Marion Keisker, who had brought him in, than with Elvis himself, whom I found, on this and a couple of other occasions, virtually un-interviewable.

Keisker had phoned me earlier that morning from Sun Records, a block up the street from my office, where she was producer/proprietor Sam Phillips' right arm. She had this promising young Sun artist she would like to bring in to see me. She thought he had something and, hopefully, would make an item for my Front Row column.

"His name is Elvis Presley," she said (the first time I had ever heard the name). "Could we come on his lunch hour — a little after 12? He drives a truck for Crown Electric Co., and that's the only time he can get away."

Edwin Howard

The Front Row
(Aug. 17, 1977)

Remembering How It All Began for Elvis . . .

THE MORNING of July 27, 1954, Marion Keisker (now Macinnes) phoned me from Sun Records, where she was Sam Phillips' right arm, and asked if she might bring a promising young Sun artist in to see me. Marion thought he had something. He had first come to Sun months before to use the studio's rental facilities to make a record for his mother on her birthday. Phillips had been intrigued and eventually recorded the boy commercially.

They would have to come in on the boy's lunch hour, Marion said, because he was still driving a truck for Crown Electric Co. I said I'd be glad to see them, and shortly after noon they got off the elevator on the fifth floor of *The Press-Scimitar* and came over to my desk.

The boy's hair looked as if it had been cut by a lawn mower, but the trademarks were already there — flat top, duck tail and sideburns. He was shy and, except for "Yes sir" and "No sir," let Marion do all the talking.

Here is the item that ran the next day in The Front Row — the first "interview" ever done with Elvis Presley:

IN A SPIN — Elvis Presley can be forgiven for going round and round in more ways than one these days. A 19-year-old Humes High graduate, he just signed a recording contract with Sun Record Co. of Memphis, and already has a disc out that promises to be the biggest hit that Sun has ever pressed.

ELVIS
First photo, 1954

It all started when Elvis dropped in to Sun's studios one day to cut a personal record at his own expense. Sam Phillips, president of the company, monitored the session and was so impressed with the unusual quality of the young man's voice that he jotted down his name and address. Some time later, Phillips came across a ballad which he thought might be right for Presley's voice. They recorded it; it didn't click. But they tried again, this time with "Blue Moon of Kentucky," a folk standard, backed by "That's All Right, Mama."

Just now reaching dealer's shelves, the record is getting an amazing number of plays on all Memphis radio stations. "The odd thing about it," says Marion Keisker of the Sun office, "is that both sides seem to be equally popular on pop, folk and race record programs. This boy has something that seems to appeal to everybody.

"We've just gotten the sample records out to the disc jockeys and distributors in other cities," she said, "but we got big orders yesterday from Dallas and Atlanta." Sun, started by Sam Phillips, former WREC engineer, several years ago, has 40 distributors from coast to coast, so there's a good chance of a big national sale.

Elvis, son of Mr. and Mrs. Vernon Presley, 462 Alabama, is a truck driver for Crown Electric Co. He has been singing and playing the guitar since he was about 13 — just picked it up himself. The home folks who have been hearing him on records so often during the past few weeks can see Elvis in person when he's presented by disc jockey Bob Neal in a hillbilly show at Overton Park Shell Friday night along with veteran entertainers from the Louisiana Hayride.

THE LATE Bob Johnson, television and later Good Evening columnist for *The Press-Scimitar*, took over the Elvis watch after that and wrote reams about him, covering his Las Vegas debut in 1955 and eventually commuting to New York to edit a magazine devoted primarily to Elvis, called *16.* I got back into the act occasionally, since I covered movies. I covered his last live show before going into the Army, and had a private interview with him in November of 1963 on the set of *Kissin' Cousins* at MGM.

"I guess the last time I really saw you was at the Tupelo Fair just before I went into the Army," he said as he sat down in his portable dressing room on the sound stage. "Gosh, an awful lot has happened since then. A lot of pictures, too. Let's see, this must be 11 since I got out.

"Yes I still enjoy it. I don't know — you get a little older and you get a little more adjusted to it. It gets to be just a job. I guess the biggest thing is the mental strain, trying to remember your lines and look your best, and all that.

"I don't have much time for anything else while I'm working. Work pretty late every night. But I do date Ann-Margret some."

THAT WAS THE LAST TIME I talked to Elvis, but of course I've kept up with him — and in recent years felt sorry for him. Not because he turned 40 and got fat. That was natural. The body matures and grows old.

What was sad to me was that imprisoned within that body was a child who never grew up. He made a huge fortune and might have done great good without depriving himself. He could have endowed hospitals, universities, research. Instead he gave nominally to varied charities and bought expensive cars for strangers — like an ordinary person tossing pennies to ragamuffins.

He might himself have traveled and studied and grown. Instead, he was content to go on playing the games of his youth — renting theaters and rinks and courts and amusements parks for private parties — playing pitch for kewpie dolls.

There was a time, after his return from Army service, when he began to blossom as an actor and might have developed into a fine one. But again he drew back and instead re-made again and again the same formula films. He never developed, never learned how to spend his money — or his time.

Middle age sat unseemly on him. Old age would have been obscene. His life had become so sad to me that his death seems less so.

Elvis Presley's first newspaper interview, on July 27, 1954, on the release of his first record, also appeared in the column the author wrote the day Elvis died.

(Memphis Press-Scimitar, August 17, 1977)

I said I'd be glad to talk to the boy, and now here they were. The boy appeared to be shy, and was certainly inarticulate. Except for a few yessirs and nosirs, he let Keisker do all the talking. But, mostly for Marion's sake, I ran an item about him, anyway. Here it is — the first "interview" with Elvis Presley ever published anywhere:

☆ ☆ ☆

IN A SPIN — Elvis Presley can be forgiven for going round and round in more ways than one these days. A 19-year-old Humes High graduate, he just signed a recording contract with Sun Record Co. of Memphis, and already has a disk out that promises to be the biggest hit Sun has ever pressed.

It all started when Elvis dropped in to Sun's studios one day to cut a personal record at his own expense. Sam Phillips, president of the company, monitored the session and was so impressed with the unusual quality of the young man's voice that he jotted down his name and address. Some time later, Phillips came across a ballad which he thought might be right for Presley's voice. They recorded it; it didn't click. But they tried again, this time with "Blue Moon of Kentucky," a folk standard, backed by "That's All Right, Mama."

Just now reaching dealer's shelves, the record is getting an amazing number of plays on all Memphis radio stations. "The odd thing about it," says Marion Keisker of the Sun office, "is that both sides seem to be equally popular on pop, folk and race record programs. This boy has something that seems to appeal to everybody.

"We've just gotten the sample records out to the disk

jockeys and distributors in other cities," she said, "but we got big orders yesterday from Dallas and Atlanta." Sun, started by Sam Phillips, former WREC engineer, several years ago, has 40 distributors from coast to coast, so there's a good chance of a big national sale.

Elvis, son of Mr. and Mrs. Vernon Presley, 462 Alabama, is a truck driver for Crown Electric Co. He has been singing and playing the guitar since he was about 13, he said — just picked it up himself. The home folks who have been hearing him on record so often during the past few weeks can see Elvis in person when he's presented by disk jockey Bob Neal in a hillbilly show at Overton Park Shell Friday night along with veteran entertainers from the Louisiana Hayride.

☆ ☆ ☆

I tried to interview Elvis again in May 1957 as he was appearing in "Jailhouse Rock" at MGM, but found the set locked up tighter than a jailhouse. I was told that Elvis took direction well (from Richard Thorpe) as long as there was nobody on the set but him and the director, cast and crew. But as soon as some outsider put in an appearance, an old friend in the MGM publicity department told me, "he begins to try to act."

As an alternative to visiting the set, my friend Ralph Wheelwright scheduled me for a lunch/interview on the lot with Elvis on May 17, but it was postponed because he had sucked a temporary tooth cap down his windpipe into his right lung and it had to be retrieved. Our date was re-set for May 21, but had to be canceled when director Thorpe ordered

Elvis to spend his lunch hours all that week studying his lines — at least that was the story they gave me — and I had to head back to Memphis.

So, unable to talk to him directly, I talked to others in Hollywood about him — to Lizabeth Scott, who had just appeared with him in "Loving You," his studio barber Ramiro Jaloma, his new friend Nick Adams, his musical director at MGM, Jeff Alexander, and well-known Paramount producer William Perlberg.

The sultry Scott told me she was "just amazed at his histrionic ability. He had a lot of really dramatic scenes, and he's just great in them. No matter what happens to music, Elvis has a future in the movies. And if he continues to improve, he'll just be a wow."

Barber Jaloma declared: "He's the greatest." I said, "Did you really cut his hair? I hear he's very particular about it."

"Yeah," Jaloma said, "I really did trim it. I said to Mr. (Hal) Wallis (the producer) when I first saw him: 'Let me at him.' And Mr. Wallis said O.K. So I told Elvis, 'Look, you can keep your sideburns and your long hair, but still look human. You know?' He argued with me a little bit, but I had the scissors. You know that duck-tail he had in the back with the hair going this way and that way? Well, I changed that to what we call a businessman's neck. And when I got through, Elvis liked it fine. We got along swell."

Adams, a young actor working in "Teacher's Pet," who was becoming one of Elvis' best friends in Hollywood and later visited him in Memphis, told me: "He's the nicest guy I've ever known. There's maybe one guy in 10 million that has that certain something that shows up on the screen and makes a real star and, believe me, Elvis has got it."

Alexander, musical director of "Jailhouse Rock," had mixed feelings about Elvis' talent. On the one hand, he said, "Elvis is a completely natural, unschooled musician. He has very, very good instincts about what is good for him. When we did the pre-recordings for the picture, I found it was better to leave him alone. . ." And then Alexander gave me a piece of history-making Hollywood news.

"For the first time in movie history, so far as I know," he said, "Our pre-recording was completely ad lib."

But then he added: "I don't think Elvis will last as a singer after rock'n'roll. He is not a performer in the sense of learning to do a thing a set way and being able to repeat it the exact same way. He is an intuitive singer, and as far as I can tell, his intuition is all in the primitive vein. As an actor, I'm told he may have what it takes to last. I wouldn't know about that. But as a musician, I doubt it."

Bill Perlberg, the crusty producer of "Teacher's Pet," had a markedly different reaction to Elvis than anyone else I talked to during the star's early years in Hollywood. I told him that, whatever they thought of his music, people out there kept telling me Elvis was so humble, so shy and modest, always answering questions with a polite "Yessir" or "Nosir," as he had me in my first interview three years before, and ma'aming all the ladies. Perlberg thought about that for a minute, and then replied with an answer I didn't even try to get printed in my '50s family newspaper.

Dragging on his cigarette and expelling a plume of smoke consideringly, he ventured: "My impression is that he's a humble shit-heel."

My next "interview" with Elvis was just four months later, on Sept. 27, 1957 — at the Mississippi-Alabama Fair in Tupelo, the town where he was born.

With the singer facing an imminent call-up in the draft (though it didn't actually happen until the following spring), his manager, Col. Tom Parker, was billing the concert as his "farewell appearance" before going into the Army, and had scheduled a "press conference" in a pyramidal tent near the outdoor stage where Elvis would be performing.

There were no signs of the old "humility" in Elvis' demeanor at this so-called press conference, which turned out in reality to be a performance for his retinue (later dubbed the "Memphis Mafia") and his and their friends, who thronged the tent along with those of us who had real press credentials.

As he strode into the tent, he had a look of prosperous-ness and self-assurance that contrasted startlingly with his appearance and manner that day he had walked into my office for his first interview just over three years before. He looked at least 20 pounds heavier and the added weight made him seem taller and more commanding. His skin was smooth — under make-up. His hair, though still long and in sideburns, was shiny black instead of mousey brown, and not a lock was out of place except an errant one trained now and then to curl down over his forehead.

His clothes were casual, but well-cut from rich fabrics — black slacks and a black cashmere sport coat over white knit sport shirt, open at the throat. A dozen or more teen-aged girls, who had wangled press passes, crowded around Elvis in the tent. He jovially signed articles of their clothing and posed for snapshots with them. Also on hand, but standing aside from the giggling girls, was his slightly older girl friend of the moment, Memphis singer and TV personality Anita Wood.

As the press conference began, Elvis sat himself on a table on one side of the tent, under the glare of a single, dangling light bulb. He smiled mischievously — some might have said arrogantly — as he answered questions about "Jailhouse Rock," the Christmas album he had just recorded in Hollywood, and the proposed Elvis Presley Youth Center in Tupelo. Many of his answers were wise-cracks, some of them jokes understood only by his retinue, who vied with each other to see who could laugh the loudest. If he had ever been truly shy and humble, he had cured himself of both. Twice during the session, he said, "I really enjoy these press conferences; they're really a lot of fun for me."

When Elvis returned from the Army two and a half years later, Col. Parker lost no time in turning him into a money-making machine. And, contrary to "Jailhouse Rock" musical director Jeff Alexander's forecast to me, he had learned to repeat himself exactly. In fact, he soon became the most proficient of all the now myriad Elvis Presley imitators.

I had one more personal encounter with him — on the set of "Kissin' Cousins," one of the cookie-cutter romantic comedies Col. Parker had him rolling out — in 1963.

To my surprise, I found him subdued and rather philosophical as we sat in his portable dressing-room on the MGM sound stage — alone, I suddenly realized, for the first time ever. Perhaps because none of his Memphis Mafiosi was around for him to perform for, I was able, for once, to have a real conversation with him.

Remembering that we had last seen each other at the fair

in Tupelo, he said, rather wearily: "Gosh, an awful lot has happened since then. A lot of pictures, too. Let's see, this must be 11 since I got out (of the Army). (His count was absolutely correct — 11 movies in just three years.)

"I still enjoy it," Elvis continued without enthusiasm. "I don't know — you get a little older and you get a little more adjusted to it. It gets to be just a job. I guess the biggest thing is the mental strain — tryin' to remember your lines and look your best, and all that. It gets to be just a job."

Not yet married to Priscilla Beaulieu, his young girl friend from Germany, although she was living in his Graceland home in Memphis, he was dating one of Hollywood's hottest sex-pots.

"I don't have much time for anything else while I'm workin'," he said. "I work pretty late every night, but I do date Ann-Margret some."

He was presumably still dating her two years later when I interviewed Ann-Margret in her gold-pink-and-chartreuse portable dressing-room on the "Made in Paris" set at MGM. It was early 1965, and after establishing what I thought was a friendly rapport with her, I mentioned her pink Cadillac convertible (pink Cadillacs had been identified with Elvis since he gave his mother one early in his career), and ventured, "Didn't I read recently where Elvis gave you a tape player for your car?"

Staring straight ahead with a fixed smile, she stonewalled me. In those repressive times, studios could break contracts with actors guilty of "moral turpitude," which for all I knew could have included accepting a pink Cadillac convertible from a man not her husband. She had stonewalled me on something as small as a tape player, so instead of asking her about the Cadillac, I asked if she were still dating Elvis.

Cutting her eyes over at me with a witchy grin, she said, "Honey, you know I ain't gonna answer any questions like that."

In 1994, on a promotional tour for her autobiography, "Ann-Margret: My Story," she finally talked a little about her relationship with Elvis.

"We talked about marriage," she told The Washington Post's Martha Sherrill. "We were so alike, so compatible. Elvis didn't like strong, aggressive women, and I posed no threat there."

In her book, she told — what was not generally known at the time — how in 1964 (several months before my interview) she began living with Roger Smith, the TV star she married in 1967. Did she move in with Roger because Elvis had Priscilla, whom he had met in Germany when she was 14, living in his house in Memphis? Was it just coincidence that the year Elvis finally married Priscilla was the year Ann-Margret finally married Roger?

Of such intimate matters, Ann-Margret did not write, even a quarter-century later, nor did she speak — even to sell her book. In it, she doesn't even tell whether she and Elvis ever kissed — and the name of Priscilla Beaulieu Presley does not appear in the book at all.

Back in Elvis' "Kissin' Cousins" dressing-room in 1963, he told me about another of his Hollywood diversions. "The fellows and I play a little football," he said. "We usually go over to Valley Junior College, not far from the house I'm leasing in Bel-Air, and play a while. That's about all the recreation I have time for."

Then he got up and went over to his dressing table and picked up a blond wig. "Isn't that awful?" he demanded. "I have to wear it in some of my scenes. You know I play two roles — an Air Force lieutenant named Josh and his mountaineer cousin named Jody, and Jody is a blond, so I have to wear the wig. When I first saw it I called the Colonel and said, 'Colonel, I'm not comin' out in this thing.' But of course I finally had to."

Another sign of Elvis' smoothed edges was his diplomatic reply when I asked him how he felt about the public controversy back home in Memphis over a proposal to name some public facility there for him:

"Well, it would be a hell of an honor, of course, but they started it without me knowing anything about it and I haven't gotten involved in it. I know it's kinda touchy." (In the end, it was the major thoroughfare in front of Graceland that was named for him, changing Bellevue Boulevard to Elvis Presley Boulevard.)

As I wound up the interview, Elvis told me he was looking forward to driving back to Memphis in time for Thanksgiving. "It'll be my first Thanksgiving at home in four years," he said. "Then right after Christmas, I have to be back out here to make another picture at Paramount, a carnival story called 'Roustabout.'"

Back out on the set, Col. Parker, an ex-carnie himself, told me with a twinkle in his eye, "I'm gonna be technical adviser on 'Roustabout.' I was also technical adviser on 'Love Me Tender' and 'G.I. Blues.' The first one, I advised him how to get to the studio. The second one, I advised him how to wear his dog tags."

Showing off for me, the Colonel then volunteered, "You

know, the other day a producer told me Elvis is slipping a little. I said yeah, I'd heard that, and the producer said, 'What's your price now?'

"I said, well, I had gone up by $100,000 a picture. He said, 'What? I just told you he was slipping.' I said, 'Yeah, that's why we got to get a little more money. We may need it.'"

Gleefully puffing on his cigar for emphasis, he added with a broad grin: "And you know what? He paid it."

"So what is Elvis' asking price now?" I asked.

"We're getting a half-million plus 50 per cent of the profits for this one," the Colonel confided. "We usually don't sling those figures around, but you asked me. I never give out phony figures, because if you do you might start believing them yourself, and then your bank account don't balance."

The Colonel did not then confide, however — as was revealed in court proceedings after Elvis' death — that he was getting 50 per cent of everything Elvis was getting.

☆ ☆ ☆

The last column I wrote about Elvis appeared Aug. 17, 1977, the day after he died, and was widely reproduced and quoted, from The New York Post to the Los Angeles Times, bringing me a bushel of mail ranging from anonymous death threats and agonized statements of sincere disagreement to a gratifying few letters of equally heartfelt agreement and praise. After reprinting my first interview and briefly recounting my other encounters with the rock'n'roll legend over the years, here is what I wrote that aroused such passions:

☆ ☆ ☆

That was the last time I talked to Elvis, but of course I've kept up with him — and in recent years felt sorry for him. Not because he turned 40 and got fat. That was natural. The body matures and grows old.

What was sad to me was that, imprisoned within that body was a child who never grew up. He made a huge fortune and might have done great good without depriving himself. He could have endowed hospitals, universities, research. Instead, he gave nominally to varied charities and bought expensive cars for strangers — like an ordinary person tossing pennies to ragamuffins.

He might himself have traveled and studied and grown. Instead, he was content to go on playing the games of his youth — renting theatres and rinks and courts and amusements parks for private parties, playing pitch for kewpie dolls.

There was a time, after his return from Army service, when he began to blossom as an actor and might have developed into a fine one. But again he drew back and instead re-made again and again the same formula films. He never developed, never learned how to spend his money, or his time.

Middle age sat unseemly on him. Old age would have been obscene. His life had become so sad to me that his death seems less so.

Chapter 9

WILLIAM FAULKNER: LIKED TO WALK IN THE DUST OF THE ROAD

For about five years before Elvis Presley rocketed to stardom in 1954, the living Mississippian most famous around the world was a country gentleman of Oxford who also wrote books. His name was William Faulkner, and although his greatest works were written between 1929 and 1942, he did not really become popular or famous prior to the publication in 1946 of Malcolm Cowley's "The Portable Faulkner," which brought together some of the best of his writings along with a brilliant analysis of his themes and style, and a lucid explanation of his mythical county of Yoknapatawpha and its capital of Jefferson, based on his own geographical center of Lafayette County and Oxford. (It might be argued that if Faulkner was of the class of decadent Southern aristocrats represented in his works by the Sartorises and Compsons, Elvis was one of the Snopeses, come to displace them.)

As interest in his work began to grow around the world, Faulkner in 1948 published the novel, "Intruder in the Dust," which proved to be the most accessible of his works up to that time. Screen rights to it were purchased by Metro-Goldwyn-Mayer for $50,000 which, even minus the $10,000 that went to his publisher Random House, was the most he had ever earned for any of his writings.

When MGM sent University of Tennessee-educated Clarence Brown, famous as Greta Garbo's favorite director, and a troupe of actors and technicians to Oxford to film "Intruder in the Dust" in the spring of 1949, Faulkner's Oxford neighbors were beginning to think he might perhaps be somewhat more respectable than they had previously believed. Prior to the late '40s, most Oxfordians had thought of him as a ne'er-do-well who quit the only job he'd ever had, as the University of Mississippi's campus postmaster, because he was tired of "being at the beck and call of every son of a bitch who's got two cents to buy a stamp," or else as a pornographer who, in "Sanctuary," had written the dirtiest book any of them had ever not read, or both.

When in 1950 Faulkner was awarded the Nobel Prize and made an eloquent acceptance speech at the award ceremonies in Stockholm, which was quoted and reprinted around the world, even his most disapproving neighbors could not fail to be impressed.

I first met Faulkner at the world premiere of "Intruder in the Dust" at the little Lyric Theatre in Oxford on Oct. 11, 1949. The event was supposed to begin with a cocktail reception and press conference in the upstairs clubroom of the restaurant next door to the theatre. None of the three veteran press agents MGM had sent out from Hollywood to run the premiere — Barrett Kiesling, Emery Austin and E.B. Coleman — really expected Faulkner, known to be shy and reclusive, to show up. But none of the film critics and columnists they had brought in from around the country was going to miss even a one-in-a-million chance that he might. Besides, the premiere party was the only place in Oxford where a stranger could get a drink.

As late-afternoon shadows fell across the front of the theatre, I stood out front watching for a Memphis Press-Scimitar photographer, the late George Pierce, to arrive to help me cover the premiere. He soon appeared, Speed Graphic in one hand, and his shoulder drooping under the weight of a huge camera bag loaded with heavy film-holders and dozens of flash bulbs.

Watching him approach, I saw that walking along behind him was a small man in an English-cut brown tweed jacket with suede patches on the elbows, rumpled cotton pants and a plain white T-shirt. The salt-and-pepper hair, coal-black mustache and one-day growth of beard plainly identified him as William Faulkner.

As I stepped forward to greet my photographer and introduce myself and him to the author and evening's honoree, Faulkner turned to Pierce, still bowed under the weight of the camera bag, and asked hospitably, in a phrase not far removed from Elizabethan English, "Can I tote that fer ye?"

Declining with thanks, Pierce started up the stairs and I got to ask Faulkner the first question of the afternoon: Why, when even the MGM people weren't really expecting him to appear, had he decided to attend the press reception?

"Well," he said, "if all you newspaper people have come to Oxford especially to see a movie made out of one of my books, it would surely be impolite of me not to walk a few blocks to meet and talk to you."

The other newsmen pounced on him the minute we reached the top of the stairs, but he seemed relieved that the press conference was going to be completely informal — completely indistinguishable, in fact, from the cocktail party.

A bar had been set up at one end of the room and there was a table loaded down with appetizing hors d'oeuvres. Almost everybody already had a glass in his hand, and the late Paul Hochuli, columnist for the Houston Press, who was widely known for the flexibility of his elbow, asked solicitously, "Can I get you a drink, Mr. Faulkner?"

A very dignified man despite the country colloquialisms of his speech, Faulkner replied: "No thank you. Just give me a little sody water."

Expressing the general surprise, Hochuli said, "Why, Mr. Faulkner, I thought you were a bourbon-and-branchwater man." The author smiled, "Yes, I reckon I am, but I go on the wagon now and then just to prove I can. A man oughtn't to let his habits get the best of him."

Amid chuckles and murmurs of agreement, I said, "When do you think you'll be getting off the wagon?"

"Oh," he said, "'long about November."

A few minutes later, Faulkner moved into another group of newsmen, and I followed along. After some discussion of the movie and its stars, Juano Hernandez, David Brian, Will Geer, Elizabeth Patterson and young Claude Jarman Jr. from

Nashville, someone asked Faulkner if he was writing anything at the moment. When he replied in the negative, I couldn't resist asking when he thought he might start writing again. I believe I was the only member of the other group around to hear the inevitable answer:

"Oh, 'long about November."

Writing under the influence thus became for years afterward my working explanation for the extraordinary complexity of Faulkner's syntax and the often dismaying length of his sentences. (Eudora Welty wrote in 1978 that "The 1600-word sentence in 'The Bear' races like a dinosaur across the early fields of time. It runs along with a strange quality of seeming all to happen at once.")

But because of that length and complexity, many have failed to hear the Gothic thunder of his prose over the rattle of his commas and semi-colons. Insofar as the style stood between the author and his readers it was a defect. But, as I wrote in an estimate of his literary position the day he died, "the virtue of that defect was the utter reality it conveyed. His style suggested that before ever picking up his pen, he had conceived (or remembered) the story whole, in minute and ramified detail. When he started writing, he was thus like an old man with total recall trying to tell how things were in his youth. He jumped around. He told the story inside out, upside down and backwards. He was impatient with words, often finding them inadequate to express his thoughts. Sometimes he would send several similar words out to do the job, stringing them together for fuller shades of meaning."

Not until Malcolm Cowley, the critic/editor responsible for "The Portable Faulkner," published "—And I Worked at the

Writer's Trade: Chapters of Literary History, 1918-1978," did I become aware of another critic seriously suggesting that Faulkner might have deliberately written under the influence of alcohol to achieve his stylistic effects.

Analyzing Faulkner's writing techniques, Cowley wrote: "Those means may never be fully explored. Possibly one of them was the dangerous expedient of drinking whisky while he wrote, at least in the early years (though he seldom mentioned drinking and writing together)."

Seldom, perhaps, and maybe not intentionally, but I heard him link them the night of the premiere of "Intruder in the Dust."

Over the next few years, Faulkner's fame and recognition continued to grow. After the Nobel Prize in 1950, he won his first National Book Award in 1951 for Collected Stories and his second in 1955 for "A Fable," which also won him his first Pulitzer.

My next chance to interview Faulkner also came in 1955, and in connection with a movie. It was at a press reception honoring him in Memphis to promote the Mid-South premiere of "Land of the Pharaohs," on which he had worked as a writer with his friend, producer/director Howard Hawks. (Earlier he had co-scenarized "To Have and Have Not" for Hawks in 1945 and "The Big Sleep" in 1946.)

The reception was held at Hotel Gayoso, the historic hotel from which General Nathan Bedford Forrest, riding his horse right into the lobby, had rousted the Yankees one night, and from the balcony of which Tennessee Williams had imagined a Cotton Carnival parade onlooker directing a wad of spit straight at "Sister Woman," riding a float, in "Cat on a Hot

Tin Roof."

This time, not only Faulkner himself showed up for the press reception; he brought along his wife Estelle and daughter Jill and her husband Paul D. Summers Jr., his writer/brother John (who spelled his last name Falkner) and his wife, and their delightful aunt, Mrs. Walter B. McLean of Memphis. (Mrs. McLean had amused the press people at the "Intruder in the Dust" reception by collaring the author and telling him, "Billy, you ought to be ashamed of yourself coming here dressed like that. Before the premiere I want you to go home and shave and put on a proper shirt and tie." He did.)

When I arrived in the Regency Room of the Gayoso, Faulkner was already there, posing for photographers in front of a big poster for "Land of the Pharaohs." After five years of fame, and some fortune, he seemed much more at ease in the spotlight.

This time he was clean-shaven and was wearing a tie with gray cotton trousers and a rumpled blue cotton coat. Every now and then he drew on a Dunhill pipe, which he confided he had once dropped in the water while fishing down home. "Didn't hurt it a bit," he said. "Just as good as ever."

Between flash-bulb flashes, he sipped from a Scotch and soda. (He never limited himself to bourbon-and-branchwater.) Before each picture, he co-operatively relinquished the glass to a Warner Bros. publicity man who thought it might not look nice to some people for him to have a drink in his hand.

As at all such affairs, there was little opportunity for sustained conversation, but I did manage to gather some lore on the author's then little-known career as a Hollywood screenwriter. (Producer Jerry Wald later told me as absolute truth, personally witnessed by him, the oft-told story that Faulkner, never very happy working in the cramped writers' buildings at the Hollywood studios, one day asked the head of the story department if he might go home to finish the script he was working on. The executive agreed, and Faulkner could not be found for some days after. He had gone home to Oxford to work instead of to his Hollywood digs.)

Faulkner had been reluctant to pass judgment on the film version of his own "Intruder in the Dust" beyond praising producer/director Brown's use of natural sounds such as cricket chirps and saddle squeaks for atmosphere "instead of a lot of loud music," but talked easily about "Land of the Pharaohs," perhaps because in it he had no personal stake (and hadn't yet seen it, anyway).

"Howard and I invented the story," he told me, "on a trip to Italy. Then Harry Kurnitz and Harold Jack Bloom put it in script form.

"Howard wanted me to go to Egypt to watch some of the filming. I went and we were there for weeks without shooting a foot of film. Political trouble. As soon as I could get out, I got!"

What did he think of the film? He was going to see it later that evening at the screening, he said, but he wasn't worried; he knew it would be good, because Hawks, his friend for 25 years, always knew what he was doing.

"'Land of the Pharaohs' is nothing new," he said. "It's the same movie Howard has been making for 35 years. It's 'Red River' all over again. The Pharaoh is the cattle baron, his jewels are the cattle, and the Nile is the Red River. But the thing about Howard is, he KNOWS it's the same movie — and he knows how to make it."

☆ ☆ ☆

My last encounter with William Faulkner was at his funeral on July 7, 1962, the day after he died of a heart attack in the hospital, to which he had been admitted the day before, still not feeling well after being thrown from his horse some 10 days before that.

A few days before he died, I had met his young protegee, author Joan Williams, at a backyard barbecue in Memphis. We had both been at Southwestern (now Rhodes College) in the late '40s, and I had recently reviewed her first published novel, "The Morning and the Evening," for which two months earlier she had been awarded the John P. Marquand First Novel Award, but this was the first time we had actually met.

We hit it off immediately, having in common the belief that Faulkner's "The Sound and the Fury" was the best novel of our time, and enthusiasm for "The Reivers," his just-published, delightfully antic picaresque novel about 11-year-old Lucius Priest's trek from Jefferson to Memphis with his family's part-Indian employee Boon Hogganbeck and family retainer Ned McCaslin in a 1905 Winton Flyer, their stay in a Memphis brothel, and other adventures climaxing with a crucial horse race. (The next year, Faulkner was awarded another Pulitzer, posthumously, for the novel, and in 1969 it was made into a charming movie, thanks in large part to the best performance of the late Steve McQueen's career.)

A few days after our meeting Joan called me, in shock over Faulkner's death, announced in the morning paper. Was I going to the funeral the next day, and could she ride down with me? I was, to cover it for my paper, and so picked her up early the next morning and had us in Oxford by 8 a.m.

It was widely known that Joan had been a protegee of Faulkner's, and she had told me at the barbecue how she had met him at his Oxford home, Rowan Oak, through her cousin Regina's husband, John Reed Holley. She had subsequently written him about her writing ambitions and eventually sent him a short story, "The Morning and the Evening," which he had sent off first to Harper's, which rejected it, and then turned

The young writer Joan Williams is pictured with William Faulkner, with whom she had a five-year love affair in the 1950's. (Photo courtesy of Joan Williams)

over to his agent Harold Ober to get published. Ober showed it to a young editor at The Atlantic Monthly named Seymour Lawrence, and he eventually published it as an "Atlantic First." Then, on the advice of another writer, Nancy Hale, she had expanded it into a short novel and, now married to Time-Life Books editor Ezra Bowen and mother of two young boys, had gotten it published by Atheneum.

Innocent as I was in those days, that was all I knew of Joan's relationship with Faulkner until 1971, when she published her novel, "The Wintering," the story of a young woman, a would-be writer, and her affair with a famous author.

As we reached the Oxford courthouse square that morning in 1962, there seemed to be a hush over the whole town. "I just saw him last Sunday," Joan had told me on the way down. "He looked fine. We sat with Mrs. Faulkner and her sister at Rowan Oak and talked for about half an hour. He said he was not writing another book, that he never writes in the summer. Oh, I just can't believe it!"

In town I drove first to the Douglas Funeral Home, where manager Richard Patton grumbled sleepily at the umpteenth inquiry about the services. "I oughtn't to tell you," he grouched. "I been up all night on this Faulkner funeral. Folks from all over wantin' to know about it."

I wanted to go to the house for the funeral service, but Joan didn't think we should. I said I had a story to write, but she was adamant and I couldn't bring myself to leave her on her own. We drove out to St. Peter's Cemetery instead, to find the grave site.

We found it, but not where we expected to. Two black gravediggers were carving Faulkner's last resting-place out of raw red clay in a bare new section of the cemetery. I thought of the Gravedigger scene in Hamlet: "How long hast thou been gravemaker?. . ." Joan wept.

"Too bad they didn't have no room in the family lot," Will Huston, one of the gravediggers, said, pointing up the hill toward the old part of the cemetery. "They's three generations of Faulkners buried back there." Suddenly I had the feeling that the cemetery was rejecting William Faulkner as so many towns-folk had rejected him over the years.

Back in town at the Rexall Drug Store we found Shelby Foote, who the next year would publish the first volume of his massive "The Civil War: A Narrative," and 30 years later become a media superstar as one of the commentators on Ken Burns's oft-repeated Civil War series on PBS, and William Styron, who five years later would publish his controversial best-seller, "The Confessions of Nat Turner." We joined them for coffee and talked about Faulkner.

Joan said, "I'll miss just knowing that he's here. It's so hard to realize that there'll be no more books from him. And yet he has left us a great body of work. I think his stature will grow."

"It's a curious thing," said Foote, who never made any bones about Faulkner's being both an idol and a model, "but a man's death seems to give shape to his whole life. The four great writers of our time — Faulkner, Fitzgerald, Wolfe and Hemingway — are gone now, and I don't think there is any question that Faulkner stands above them all, both for the volume and quality of his work."

With the same sagacious insight and perspicacity he would later demonstrate on PBS, talking about Stonewall

Faulkner's death in 1962 was so sudden that his grave was still being dug the morning of his funeral in Oxford, Miss. (Author's collection)

Faulkner's Oxford home, Rowan Oak, shown decorated for Christmas, is now a museum, open to the public. (Author's collection)

Jackson or Robert E. Lee, Foote concluded: "He always reached beyond himself. He was not always successful, but his work was greater because of the things he was willing to try."

I suggested that his success rate was pretty high, at that;

I could think of no other Southern writer who had come close to him.

Foote grinned his agreement: "I think it was Flannery O'Connor who said, when somebody asked if the Faulkner influence bothered her, 'When you hear the Dixie Special coming down the line, you'd better get off the track."

I didn't record any comment by Styron; as usual, Foote had said it all.

Leaving the drug store, we got outside just in time to see a black Cadillac hearse taking Faulkner for his last ride around the courthouse square of Jefferson, county seat of Yoknapatawpha, of which he was owner and sole proprietor.

It was now about an hour until the home funeral service, which Joan felt we should not attend, and which I had now learned was closed to the press, anyway. So instead of listening to the tape the Rt. Rev. Duncan Gray Jr., who would conduct the service, had made of the burial office from the Book of Common Prayer, as the rest of the press contingent was doing, I decided to use the time to conduct some research into the relative amounts of truth and fiction in "The Reivers," and Joan was glad to accompany me on the quest.

My best source, I had been told, would be Earl Wortham, the African-American blacksmith who took care of the Faulkner horses. I found him in a little shack out east of town on State Highway 6 and got a tantalizing glimpse not only into some Faulkner family history that he had transmogrified into "The Reivers," but also into the character of Faulkner himself.

"Yessir," Wortham told me. "I been shoein' horses for Mr. Bill 10 or 15 years, I reckon, and I knowed him since he was a little boy about that high." (He held his hand about three feet off the ground.)

"He was a fine little boy, but he was always different. They had a nurse for him and the other children they called 'Nanny.' I 'member she used to walk 'em downtown and all the children would walk on the board sidewalk 'cept little Bill. She'd say, 'Get up here on this sidewalk, Billy,' and he'd say, 'I ain't gonna do it,' and he wouldn't. I don't know why, but he liked to walk in the dust of the road.

"I worked for Mr. Bill's daddy at his livery stable. My daddy hired me out to him for 50 cents a day. Mr. Bill, he always loved to ride. Lately, I been gettin' on him — a man his age ridin' and jumpin' the way he did! Sometimes one of them horses would come out from under him. I reckon it was about two weeks ago one of 'em throwed him, and he didn't look like he felt like hisself since.

"I didn't hear 'bout him bein' dead till I come home yesterday evenin'. Mr. Fred, up at the store, he told me he heard it but didn't know if it was true. Then Mrs. McClaherty called and said it was.

"Mr. Bill was the finest kind of a man to work for. I never did see him get mad once. We sure are goin' to miss him."

On a hunch I asked Wortham if he knew Faulkner's last novel, "The Reivers," was about a horse race.

"Yessir," he grinned, "he told me he was writin' somethin' about a race up in Tennessee."

I told him the story began at a livery stable, probably the very one where he used to work for 50 cents a day, and maybe he was in the book. He just laughed.

A boy and his cousin and a black man drove a 1905 automobile to Memphis, I told him, and traded it for a race horse in the story. "Did you ever drive a car to Memphis when you were a kid?

"Nossir, I didn't," he said earnestly, "but Chester Carothers did.

"He was the Colonel's driver. The Colonel was Mr. Bill's granddaddy. The Colonel's car was made right here in town out of an old buggy. A man named John Buffalo — used to live right up there on the hill — built it."

I asked Wortham if Chester Carothers still lived in Oxford and he said no, he thought he might be still living, but he had gone to Memphis some years ago. A few days after my story appeared in The Memphis Press-Scimitar I got a call from a man who thought he knew where Chester Carothers worked. I found the man, whose name was indeed Carothers and who had moved up from Oxford several years before, but he turned out to be Chester Carothers' son. Although he remembered his daddy talking about driving to Memphis in a home-made car many years before, he could add nothing to what Earl Wortham, the Faulkner family blacksmith, had told me.

Joan and I went back to the cemetery and observed the burial from a discreet distance. I caught sight of Bennett Cerf entering the graveside marquee. We drove to her cousins Regina and John Reed Holley's house and I set up my portable in the backyard, wrote my story, and phoned it in for the afternoon edition. Then we drove back to Memphis, mostly in silence.

We have kept up with each other over the years. Joan went on to write "Old Powder Man," "The Wintering," and

"County Woman," all of which I reviewed. In 1980, she wrote a touching eight-page memoir of her five-year affair with Faulkner for The Atlantic Monthly. She couldn't believe that I didn't know the nature of her relationship with Faulkner until I read her fictionalization of it in "The Wintering." She divorced and remarried. She divorced again, and Seymour Lawrence, the editor who published her original short story version of "The Morning and the Evening," came back into her life, 30 years later, at a PEN/Faulkner Writers' Conference. By now he was one of the country's most successful and respected independent publishers, associated with Houghton-Mifflin. "Sam (Seymour) and I had a fantastic life together," she told me recently — until he died suddenly in early 1994. They had owned a house together in Connecticut, and in April of 1993 they had moved into a house he had bought in Oxford, right across the street from Rowan Oak, the house, now a museum, where Faulkner, once her mentor/lover, whom Lawrence also greatly respected, had lived.

After Lawrence's death, Joan Williams left Oxford and Rowan Oak and moved back to Memphis, where she trained to work in a downtown street ministry to the homeless. Later, she and her son Matt moved to Charlottesville, Va., where Faulkner had spent time as a writer-in-residence at the University of Virginia.

Chapter 10

JOHN GRISHAM: LAWYER WITH THE WRITE STUFF

Even after he died (and he did die), Elvis Presley remained the most famous "living" Mississippian around the world until the summer of 1993 when a handsome young Southaven, Miss., lawyer and legislator named John Grisham suddenly displaced him. He did this not by rotating his pelvis, strumming a guitar, or bleating a rock'n'roll lament, but by selling, each and every day for 18 months, more than five times as many copies of his first four novels as were accounted for by William Faulkner's first four novels over their entire shelf life.

Grisham's sales during that 18 months were averaging more than 46,000 copies a day of "The Firm," "A Time to Kill," "The Pelican Brief," or "The Client." Although Faulkner would eventually win two Pulitzer Prizes and a Nobel Prize among numerous other awards, the dapper little gentleman's first four novels averaged sales of only 2,000 each (8,000 total), and the highest any of his books ever got on a bestseller list was No. 10 for "The Reivers," published just before he died in 1962. With "The Firm," John Grisham became the best-selling brand name in publishing.

I first interviewed Grisham in July, 1993 (39 years after my first interview with Elvis in July, 1954, and 44 years after my first interview with Faulkner in October, 1949), and found him more articulate than either, and still refreshingly awed by his own success.

By this time, Grisham, his wife Renee, and their son Ty and daughter Shea had moved from Southaven, a suburb of Memphis, to a big Victorian-style house they had built on 70 acres of rich Mississippi farmland on the outskirts of Oxford, where Faulkner's home, Rowan Oak, is now a museum, and his name is as revered as it was often ridiculed during his lifetime.

Of Grisham's new life and fortune (he doesn't like to talk about his finances, but he had already earned about $25 million from his writing on those first four books), he told me with a kind of gee-whiz candor: "I feel like the luckiest person in the world. I never have to work again in my life. I really don't think it's gone to my head, though. I wake up every morning and I thank God for all these unbelievably wonderful things that have happened to me. It has brought Renee and me and the kids closer together, because there are moments when the pressures from the outside really get to us. Then we sort of retreat to ourselves, take a trip, or lock the gate and play on the farm."

Knowing that he had earned his law degree at Ole Miss, where Faulkner had flunked out in his second year, and that, like Faulkner, he had created his own mythical county for his first novel, "A Time to Kill," I asked Grisham about his literary models, if any.

"I've always had a lot of admiration for John Steinbeck," he said. "I had a high school English teacher at Southaven (Miss.) High School who exposed me to the great American authors, and John Steinbeck was one who really struck a nerve with me. I really enjoyed his books. I remember reading 'The Grapes of Wrath' and 'Of Mice and Men' and thinking, 'Gosh, I wish I could write that clearly.'

"At the same time, we were reading Faulkner, so I really appreciated Steinbeck's clarity. Much easier to read ."

"So Faulkner," I proposed, "was not a role model for you, but more of a bad example?"

Sounding far less unkind than the way in which I had framed the question, he said, "Yeah, in that his writing was so convoluted, and after law school I was determined to write as clearly and simply and straightforwardly as I possibly could.

"In our law schools, we aren't trained to write that way. We're trained to use 10 words when three will do just fine, and to write four-page letters when two paragraphs will do. It's just the way lawyers are trained, and it's really sad. When I started practicing law 12 years ago in Southaven, I remember listening to other lawyers drone on in the courtrooms — repeat themselves, you know. And I said to myself, 'I'm going to be very efficient with my words —written words and spoken words.' I don't know how that affected the writing of the novels exactly, but I think it did ."

More than a year before this first full-dress interview with John, I had been put in touch with him by a mutual friend, an Oxford native who was doing special assignments for the first Bush White House, and had done some research for the author on the Washington backgrounds of "The Pelican Brief." Before writing my review of that novel, I talked to him briefly on the phone about its plot, which I had found so timely as to be almost scary, tapping into so many recent headlines that it was hard to believe he had plotted the outline a year and a half earlier. That was long before the hearings on Clarence Thomas's nomination to the U.S. Supreme Court were televised, and long before Oliver Stone's "JFK" brought assassination conspiracy theories back into vogue. Yet "The Pelican Brief," of course, is jump-started by the conspiratorial assassinations of two Supreme Court justices.

Thanks to our mutual friend, Grisham told me, he had had the opportunity of going into the Oval Office on a Sunday, all by himself. He had stood there, he said, and thought about the Nixon tapes of all the Watergate plotting and covering up that had gone on in that room.

"I thought to myself," Grisham told me, "if all of that could go on inside this historic place of trust and duty, then there was not anything that I could not write and make people believe. It was very liberating for me as a writer."

In all the conversations I had with him over a period of three years, Grisham never used the word art. He called what he does "commercial fiction." His publisher, Doubleday, calls his books "legal thrillers."

The press run for his first book, "A Time to Kill," bought by Wynwood Press for $15,000, was 5,000 copies, and John bought 1,000 of them himself. But when Dell brought it out in paperback after the success of "The Firm," it stayed on the bestseller lists for 63 weeks, and sold over 10.5 million copies. And in the summer of 1994, Grisham finally sold film rights to "A Time to Kill" for "not less than $6 million" (plus $25,000 for St. Jude Children's Research Hospital in Memphis), reputedly the highest price ever paid for theatrical motion picture rights to a novel up to that time.

What made it so much more valuable in 1994 than it was in 1989? Ten and a half million readers, of course. Publishers may or may not be able to recognize a bestseller in manuscript. But Hollywood figures 10.5 million readers can't be wrong.

When I talked to John in July of 1993, The Washington Post had just run a feature on him headed, "HOT HOT HOT! WHAT'S HE GOT?" The author had declined to talk to Post Style writer David Streitfeld for the story, so I asked him if he could answer Streitfeld's question for me. What HAS he got?

"You have to go back to the four books themselves," he began. "Forget my name, and look at the books. They all have certain elements in common — ordinary people suddenly caught up in some kind of diabolical plot, and forced to run for their lives, or fight for their lives. They're very, very suspenseful. They're episodic, gripping, and hard to put down.

"And timing was very important. But it was just luck, blind luck. There was a void in commercial fiction of this type. Robert Ludlum had owned the market for many years. Ken Follett had written this kind of book, but he's English. So I think the market was just ready for a new, American suspense novelist. The market was right. The timing was right. But I didn't know it. It just happened."

How long, I wondered, did he think it might last?

"I can't see beyond five years," he said. "I can see a book a year for the next five years." (As this chapter is being written, he has completed nine or ten more books in as many years, and is still going strong.) But it may go on for 20 years. I don't know. I just don't know what I'm gonna do.

"Renee and I spend hours talking to each other about all this stuff, because there's nobody else we can talk to. Nobody we know has ever been through anything like this. There are other people who have gotten famous and made a bunch of money real fast, but I don't know 'em, and I can't go talk to 'em.

"We can't go to our parents, because they've never been through it. We can't go check out a book at the library and read how to handle it. So really, we just lean on each other."

Among the things Grisham has had the most trouble dealing with are the media, the mail, and the books people began piling by his gate to be signed. As Streitfeld wrote in his Post piece: "Every journalist in America wants to talk to him, every reader wants to meet him, and meanwhile he's only five chapters into his fifth book . . . It wasn't possible to interview him for this story . . . ."

The next interview I was able to arrange with John was in April, 1994, just after he had finished that fifth book, "The Chamber," and shipped it off to Doubleday. In February, northern Mississippi had had a devastating ice storm. When I asked him how he and his family and their 70 acres had weathered the storm, he said, almost gleefully:

"We were very lucky. We were without power for only four days, but we were without telephones for two weeks. It was wonderful! I was trying to finish 'The Chamber,' and having no phones for two weeks was the best thing that could have happened to me personally."

Just as he had spent a few quiet moments alone in the Oval Office while researching "The Pelican Brief," Grisham told me he had visited Death Row in the Mississippi State Penitentiary at Parchman for "The Chamber," not once, but several times. Oval Office, Death Row — what's the difference?

"When you've been in the Oval Office once, you really don't have to go back, it leaves such an impression," he said. "But I went back several times to Parchman, and each time I learned more about the many aspects of an execution."

As I, and numerous other, reviewers pointed out, "The Chamber" rises above the thriller genre with an extraordinarily timely and detailed analysis of one of society's most perplexing problems — crime, and its punishment. I asked the author how he himself felt about the death penalty. He said, "I was very much in favor of the death penalty before I started the book, but I'm now very ambivalent. I'm uncomfortable discussing it."

As omniscient narrator of "The Chamber," the author takes no stand on the issue, but he presents the daily life of a Death Row inmate in his 6x9-foot windowless cell (from which he is allowed out only an hour a day), the seemingly endless appeal process, and the execution ritual itself with such intensity and detail that the novel's description of the carrying out of the death sentence becomes a powerful argument against it. Whatever a reader's conviction before reading it, "The Chamber" will shake it.

While the narrative landscape of "The Chamber" ranges across half of Mississippi to Memphis, Chicago and New Orleans, I was glad to find that its psychology was firmly rooted in the rich, blood-drenched soil of Grisham's mythical

Ford County, in which his first, and his own favorite, novel, "A Time to Kill," was set. On the basis of the heightened thematic importance and narrative complexity of his fifth novel and the years for growth and development still ahead for John Grisham, I believe that one day literary historians will find it important to note that he carved his mythical Ford County and town of Clanton out of the very same fields, woods, meadows and town square as Faulkner's Yoknapatawpha County and its county seat, Jefferson.

As for the media, John says, "I've been burned by so many journalists, I've gotten to the point where I just say, why bother? I'm almost afraid to talk to them. They always print something negative, no matter what I say. I've done TV a few times because at least on TV you're there on tape and it's harder for them to misconstrue what you're trying to say." He might have added, but did not, that he doesn't need the journalists, anyway. It is his name, John Grisham, now always bigger than the title, that sells his books, not reviews or interviews.

One thing he can't do without, of course, is readers, and although he is very much aware of that, and enjoys meeting them at the Square Book Store in Oxford, Burke's Book Store in Memphis, and a half-dozen other stores in the Southeastern U.S. when each new book appears, he wants no more coast-to-coast tours with their six-hour book-signing sessions in city after city.

During the summer of 1994, Grisham and his family also began to weary of the constant siege of fans at their big yellow house just outside Oxford. John could hardly believe people would come knocking on their door at all hours of the day, many of them arriving on tour buses, not to mention the volume of books left by his mail box for signing.

"I never expected all this," he said. "If I had, I wouldn't have built the house so close to the highway. I'd've built it on the back 40."

Since he couldn't move the house, he had a gate and guard tower built instead, and when even they failed to give him the privacy he not only wanted, but absolutely required to do his work, he and his family left Oxford the second week in August of 1994 and lighted out for a 200-year-old plantation house on 188 acres outside Charlottesville, Va., which he and Renee had bought 14 months earlier as a hideaway.

When he first told me about buying it — at a price The Washington Post reported at $1.2 million — he had referred to it as "a refuge — a place where we can hide out, where nobody knows we're coming and nobody knows we're there."

He said they planned to use it as a second home. "We'll probably come up here three or four times a year," he told me. "It's an old house on a little (sic) farm. Charlottesville (seat of the University of Virginia and location of Thomas Jefferson's home, Monticello) is just a wonderful area. It's so pretty, and has a great literary environment."

He knew, of course, that Faulkner had been writer-in-residence at the university in his later years. Faulkner's daughter and literary executor, Jill, lives there now.

And so, in August 1994, the Grishams' second home became their primary residence. Just at the time they were moving, but not knowing of the move until a little later, I decided it was about time for me to do another interview with America's most-read, best-paid author, and sent him a request through the private channel of communication we had agreed upon.

About three weeks later, I received the following missive in the mail :

Dear Edwin:

Good to hear from you again. We are in Virginia for the school year, and I am in seclusion trying to write the next novel. Let's wait a bit on the next interview. I've stopped talking to virtually everybody except you and maybe one or two others. I should be finished with 'The Rainmaker' by Christmas, at least that's what I promised my publisher.

Delighted you and your wife enjoyed 'The Client.' I agree. I think it's the best (film) adaptation of mine yet. Keep in touch. Best wishes.

Sincerely,

John

I did. I gave him a breather after Christmas and his presumed completion of "The Rainmaker." However, when my Feb. 27 request for another interview, sent to him through my regular channel, brought no reply over the next month, I assumed he was running a bit late with "The Rainmaker," and waited until the end of March before trying to contact him again. When the novel was published April 12, I bought it, read it, liked it, reviewed it in my column in the Memphis Business Journal, and sent him copies.

Harriet Beeson, proprietor of Burke's Book Store in

Memphis, wrote me: "Your review of 'The Rainmaker' really gives John Grisham legitimacy as an author, and it was such fun to read, as well. I've sent it to John in case he hasn't already seen it." He was due at Burke's to sign copies of "The Rainmaker" the first week in May, and Beeson's message came on a postcard bearing a photograph of the 120-year-old book store. Atop the store was a huge billboard with a picture of Grisham and the message in big red letters: "Grisham is coming!" Still no word from Grisham himself, but maybe when he finds out I've legitimized him . . . .

Then on May 15 the phone rang, I answered, and a familiar, friendly voice said, "Edwin? It's John. Sorry I haven't been able to get back to you sooner, but I've been real busy."

At my request, instead of setting up our usual taped telephone interview for a day or two hence, we agreed on a date and place for me to interview him — face to face for the first time — in Charlottesville. I didn't even ask if I could visit him at the Grishams' country retreat in Albemarle County. I know how much their privacy means to them, and I didn't want to put him on the spot.

So we met for lunch at the charming Boar's Head Inn on the southwestern edge of town, which had become for John in Charlottesville what Hotel Peabody was for him in Memphis — a place to dine, meet friends, conduct business.

I was waiting in the Club Room — between the lobby and the Old Mill Room restaurant — when he arrived, and of course it didn't take Sherlock Holmes to identify him.

A handsome 6-footer, he has what my wife calls "Paul Newman-blue eyes," tousled, short brown hair, and a receding hairline I wouldn't have noticed if he hadn't mentioned it when

John Grisham is interviewed by the author in Charlottesville, Va.
(Author's collection)

I was taking his picture. He shucked his tweed jacket, rolled up the sleeves of his bold, blue-striped, button-down shirt, and we got down to business.

Because of the conversational drone of a busload of tourists in the Old Mill Room, I had arranged for us to be served privately in the Club Room, which was fine with John. He was obviously known to hotel staff, but hotel guests let him alone.

"The Rainmaker" had been out less than six weeks when we met, but the first printing of 2.8 million copies was virtually sold out (300,000 copies sold the first week), and a second printing had been ordered by Doubleday. I asked for details on his sale of the film rights.

"As I told you on the phone," he began, "we've made a

deal with Michael Douglas and his partner Steve Reuther (formerly with New Regency, which produced the film version of "The Client" and bought film rights to "A Time to Kill.") They have financing from some Europeans."

What he hadn't told me was that instead of going for more money up front than he got for "A Time to Kill" — a record $6 million — he had decided to gamble on a percentage with "The Rainmaker." This was just at the time Winston Groom, on whose book the blockbuster "Forrest Gump" had been based, was complaining that, even though the film had already grossed over $660 million worldwide, he had yet to receive any of the 3 per cent of net profits called for in his contract. Paramount was still recording the film as $62 million in the red. I asked Grisham if Hollywood percentages didn't make him nervous.

"I'm not talking about net," he explained patiently. "I'm talking about gross — a percentage of the worldwide box office gross, which is a figure everybody is either honest about, because that's how they brag on how well the film is doing, or else, with a big movie, they may even inflate it. So we've got language in the contract inches thick assuring that it's percentage of the gross — not net profit — that I'll get. It's exciting to get plugged in from day one and dollar one."

Well, yes. That was the deal Tom Hanks had on "Forrest Gump," and even as John and I spoke, Hanks had already collected about $31 million on his way to an expected total of about $40 million for being a Gump.

I decided John had become a lot more sophisticated, if not blasé, about money than he was when I had first interviewed him two years before and he was still geewhizzing over his first millions in book royalties.

So what does he worry about? His next Little League game. I knew that, as he did in Oxford, he was coaching his son Ty's team in Charlottesville, and asked how they were doing.

"We've won six and lost five," Grisham said. "For me, .500 is great. I never play .500 ball. I've got a good team, and 12 great kids. They're 9 through 12, and they're all a delight to coach. No bad kids. No bad attitudes. They're just fun. Winning is overrated. We just like to play."

Had the move to Charlottesville, I wondered, worked out as well in other respects? Why had they really left Oxford? Was it just for a year? How had Ty and Shea adjusted? When did they plan to move back?

Grisham ruminated earnestly on the answers:

"It was strictly for privacy so I could finish 'The Rainmaker'. I love Oxford, and it'll always be my home, but it had got so there were too many distractions there. Moving wasn't easy. The older kids get, the harder it is. We knew if we didn't do it last August we'd never do it. Both our kids had been in Oxford for four years, and both were about to move to different schools, across town and all that. So they were moving, anyway, and that helped.

"It has been a wonderful year. We live about 25 miles south of here, just barely in Albemarle County. The house cannot be seen from any road. It's an old plantation house — 250 years old — and if you don't know where it is, you can't find it. We have been there for nine months, and we have yet to have the first person pull up in the drive and knock on the door and want something, which was a daily occurrence in Oxford.

"That's the difference between living here and living

Grisham's "The Firm" and "The Pelican Brief" in a Vienna bookstore window. (Author's collection)

there. It's strictly a matter of privacy. We've all adjusted very well. The kids are happy — homesick at times, but happy. And we go back to Oxford about once a month. We'll spend half the summer there. Christmas and Thanksgiving we spent there. Our best friends are there. Our kids have made wonderful friends here, but they've still got a lot of friends there. So we go back all the time.

"We have an airplane — a Cessna Citation jet, and it'll fly from the airport here to the airport in Oxford in two hours. With a good tail wind, we can do it in two hours, porch to porch. We also use the plane to bring grandparents here, and friends. The plane has made all the travel bearable. It's an eight-passenger, and it'll do 500-plus miles an hour, so we use it all the time. When I had to go to New York on business last week, I flew direct from the airport here, cutting out a lot of hassle.

"The plane stays in Memphis. If I'm not using it, it's available for charter. Your checklist of Memphis corporations use it periodically. We have two pilots dedicated to the plane, so wherever it goes, they go. They manage it, they fly it, and they take care of it. They're like members of the family. If it should be booked and we suddenly need it — it's never happened because we try to plan ahead — but if it did happen, I would just call another charter service, here or in Richmond, and order a plane.

"So the move has been good. We still ask ourselves how long we're going to be here. It's still got that temporary air to it."

Could the author see himself using Charlottesville as the setting for a future novel?

"I have not yet found any inspiration to use this area,"

he said. "Washington is irresistible, of course, when it comes to law and politics. It's a fabulous city. For all its terrific problems, it's still a fascinating place."

What was it about Charlottesville, I wondered, that did NOT inspire writers. William Faulkner lived in Charlottesville as writer-in-residence at the University of Virginia for several years, and short story master Peter Taylor lived and taught there for many years, yet — except for Taylor's last novel, "In the Tennessee Country," in which Charlottesville figured tangentially — neither ever wrote about it. I had to tell John what Taylor said when I asked him years ago why he continued to write so much about Memphis, where he actually lived only a few years, instead of about Virginia and Virginians.

"You know what Faulkner said about Virginia, don't you?" Taylor had asked me rhetorically. "Faulkner said, 'I love Virginians. They're all so snobbish, they leave you alone.'

"They're marvelous people," Taylor had continued with a touch of irony, "but there's this feeling that, yes, you're Southern, but you're not Virginian."

Grisham said he had heard the Faulkner story.

"And I'll say this," he added. "They have not been snobbish to us, but they WILL leave you alone. They're as friendly as we'll let 'em be. We haven't sought any relationships. We came here to be ignored, and left alone. But we have two kids in school, and you've got to live a life, and we've certainly done that. The Charlottesville people are great people, and we've made a lot of friends. But Charlottesville is like any university town; it's transient, like Oxford, with the University of Mississippi. People come here from everywhere. That's what I love about university towns."

Since the vitriol quotient in reviews of Grisham's books and the movies made therefrom seems to rise in direct proportion to the number of books he has sold, I asked him how he was handling all the mean-spirited criticism of his work.

"I tell Doubleday, 'Stop sending me all these stinkin' reviews,'" he said. "Life's much simpler and nicer if I don't read them. Pat Conroy gets butchered at times. They're all out after Larry McMurtry these days. William Styron even got nasty reviews of 'Sophie's Choice.'

"I knew it was time to stop reading the bitter ones when I realized I could read 19 good ones, then just one bad one and I'd want to take out after somebody with a baseball bat.

"But you know what I tell myself? I tell myself I could be back in DeSoto County Court House in Hernando, Miss., fighting over divorces and DUIs and stuff like that. So I take the criticism, because that's part of it. If I wasn't selling my books by the millions, they wouldn't be saying all those ugly things about me."

The truth is, many more people say nice things about his work than say bad things, but they are just the ordinary people who buy his books — not the critics who get them free. He gets about 50 letters a day from people telling him how much they like his books. Many also send him presents, and pictures of people they have come across reading his books in foreign lands, where they have titles like "Die Firma," "Die Akte," "Appello" and "Camara de Gas."

What kind of person is he? From my limited professional association with him as book reviewer and columnist over three years, during which we had more than five hours of concentrated conversation, he struck me as a keen observer, a quick and incisive judge of people and situations, a warm and loyal friend to friends who remain loyal to him.

I believe he is a skilled and conscientious craftsman with words and ideas who wishes he could take time to write better novels than he does. I think he has chafed a bit under the requirements of his book-a-year contract with Doubleday. He told me: "'The Chamber' was a book I loved writing. I kept saying to myself, 'I wish I had two years to write this book. I wish I had time to do it justice.'" He spent several years writing "A Time to Kill" and is still prouder of it than any other. He agreed with me that "The Chamber" was his most important book to date.

Although his books seem increasingly to be critic-proof (like Balzac's and Dickens'), and he tries not to care about mean-spirited reviews and commentaries on his career, he does care. One of these years, he is going to write a novel that will confound his critics. (When I told him I thought it was important for him to maintain a continuity of Ford County novels, he said, "I think I'll be going back there pretty soon." "The Painted House," a complete departure from his legal thrillers, and set in the rural Arkansas in which he grew up, seemed to me a thrust in that direction.)

One of the chief sources of Grisham's success as a writer is his restless, searching energy. He answers questions looking you straight in the eye, like a defense attorney (which he started out to be) intent on convincing you of his particular truth. But when you are asking him the questions, his eyes may be roaming, checking out the rest of the room, the corridor beyond. He has a mind that needs to be doing several things at once — like writing a new novel and the screenplay for his last novel at the same time.

With umpteen million dollars in the bank, I think he still has something to prove — that popularity and literary quality are not necessarily mutually exclusive, as many snooty and envious book reviewers seem to think.

Grisham would be the last person to claim kinship with the Bard, but it is worth remembering that Shakespeare, who had one of his characters in Henry V inquire sardonically of another, " .·. . art thou base, common, and popular?", was in his own time, and remains, the most popular, as well as the best, author who ever wrote. And that Shakespeare wrote for money.

Chapter 11

MARTIN SHEEN: WE'RE ALL IN THIS TOGETHER

When Charlie Sheen won the 2001 Golden Globe for best actor in a TV comedy series for "Spin City," it was Martin Sheen who took top honors with me. Charlie's father was also nominated in the drama category in '01 for "The West Wing." He didn't win that night, but he cheered louder than anybody when Charlie won.

The previous year, Martin Sheen and "The West Wing" had been the big drama winners, but as Dad cheered son at the '01 ceremonies, lip-readers could see him saying, "We got ours last year!" And many of us, familiar with Charlie's tours on the rehab circuit, could surmise his father's deeper paternal thoughts, as well.

Awards are likely to keep coming for Martin Sheen who, after an up-and-down movie career of more than 30 years, seems very much at home in "The West Wing," which has also become home for thinking television viewers.

The father-and-son successes of the Sheens sent my thoughts ranging back to 1987 when I interviewed Martin Sheen at the world press preview of director John Schlesinger's psychological thriller, "The Believers."

By that time, all three of his sons and his daughter had launched acting careers, so I asked him if he had set out to found an acting dynasty.

"My, my, no," he laughed. "I have to confess that I was always last to find out. When Emilio was in his senior year in high school, he announced that he had written a play with a colleague, and would we come down and see them act it. So my wife and I went down there and we saw this young man whom I had loved as a friend and worshipped as a son, and now came to respect as a fellow actor. How do you deal with that? I don't know. And it's been one of them after another. I'm delighted that they have a creative instinct, and they are having success with their careers, but my, my, my! I promise you that I had nothing to do with it.

"In fact, I thought all the precarious locations we had dragged them to all over the world might have the opposite effect. I thought they'd have a bellyful and never want to be involved in the movies. It's amazing. There's Emilio, Charlie, Ramon and Renee — they're all in acting."

I asked if we could get the matter of the Sheen children's names straight. Martin Sheen, Ohio-born son of a Spanish father and Irish mother, had never legally changed his real name, which is Ramon Estevez. I knew Emilio had kept Estevez, while Charlie, who had starred the previous year in

Oliver Stone's Oscar-winning "Platoon," had taken Sheen.

"My middle son, Ramon," the father said, "split the difference. He uses Ramon and Sheen. But Renee uses Estevez. So we've got Emilio Estevez, Ramon Sheen, Charlie Sheen, and Renee Estevez. Can you figure it out?"

Long before Martin Sheen became President Bartlett in "The West Wing," he had become a political activist. His activism had begun, he said, soon after he went to India in 1981 to take a major role in Richard Attenborough's "Gandhi," which made an eight-Oscar sweep of the 1982 Academy Awards.

"'Ghandi' spun my head around," he told me. "I began to see in the poverty and deprivation of India the faces of my own children. We all are indeed connected. It made a powerful impression on me. I was never the same. And I would suggest that anyone who wants to change his life radically go to India."

There's a lot of Martin Sheen in President Bartlett, and Martin Sheen was seen as presidential timber long before he made President in the TV series. In 1983, soon after returning from India, he played the late President John F. Kennedy in the TV mini-series, "Kennedy." Although he may have stood short of Kennedy's physical stature, he certainly rose to the martyred President's height histrionically.

Over a decade later, Sheen's presidential timber was tested again when he played chief-of-staff to Michael Douglas's President in director Rob Reiner's popular film, "The American President," with a script by "West Wing" writer-producer Aaron Sorkin.

My meeting with Martin Sheen came about 20 years after his motion picture career had begun. One of his first noteworthy films was "The Subject Was Roses," in which he played the son of my high school classmate, Patricia Neal, in her first screen appearance after suffering a debilitating stroke. (See chapter on her.)

But in 1987, I was more interested in the outspoken Sheen's political activism, which then centered on U.S. policies in Central America and particularly Nicaragua. These were the days of what came to be called the Iran-Contra scandal, involving both then President Ronald Reagan and Vice President George H. W. Bush, and Sheen was angry about U.S. involvement there.

That day in Toronto, with a group of film critics and columnists who had come to hear him talk about a film called "The Believers," he talked most about his own beliefs, and at this point, he demanded of several of us together at a table: "Who dies first — the assassin or the assassinated? I maintain it is the assassin, because you must be dead in order to kill — dead spiritually, I mean.

"You know my son Charlie's film, 'Platoon,' brought this home to us very clearly in regards to Vietnam veterans who engaged in some very horrible activities while they were in Vietnam. But as I watched that film, I became more and more aware that I probably would have done exactly what they did, in order to stay alive. It boils down to our humanity — or lack of it. What are we willing to do to impose ourselves on other people?"

After Sheen's passionate declarations of his political and humanitarian beliefs — his rare (for an actor) exposure of his political conscience — I couldn't resist asking my next question: Had he ever thought of running for office?

"I've fantasized about it," he replied with a smile, "but thank God I've never taken myself seriously as a potential public official. I have a public life, but I don't have a constituency. I have to answer only to my conscience.

"Mind you, I'm in love with all the accouterments of the flesh. I love to smoke — though I keep trying to quit. (As it was in 1987 with Sheen, so it is today with President Bartlett.)... I love my cars and my pool. And the love of all these earthly gifts makes it that much more difficult to hear the voice inside me.

"Not that these things are good or bad in themselves. But when they control us, make us so comfortable that we are uncomfortable in the spirit, that's the time to change.

"I think each of us must unite the will of the spirit with the work of the flesh. That's what we're here for — to become human. If you would be spiritual, be human. That's all any of the great masters have tried to teach us. They remain in the flesh, and teach us how to do it.

"Unfortunately, most of them are assassinated for doing this. All our heroes are murdered for it, but that's what we are given to aspire to — to live faithfully to ourselves."

Remembering that Sheen had donated his "Gandhi" salary to Mother Theresa, I asked if he had met her while he was over there, and another, very human, side of this remarkable citizen/actor emerged.

"Well, yes," he said, "I did donate my salary. I'm sorry that ever got out — and I wasn't the only one in the film who did this, mind you. A whole bunch of us did, and it went in a lump sum to Mother Theresa.

"I'll tell you another story in connection with that if you want. While we were in Bombay, members of the film company, as a result of that donation, were invited to go and meet her in Calcutta. We were told we should take the train on Saturday, arriving late Saturday night, and that we would then rise early on Sunday morning and attend the 5:30 mass at the Mother House, and that Mother Theresa attends that mass, and would meet us afterward. We'd actually have the chance to meet this magnificent human being.

"So when we got the invitation, I rushed back to the hotel to my son Emilio, who was traveling with me and working as a stand-in in the film, and I said, 'Emilio, guess what! We're going to meet Mother Theresa!' And I excitedly told him the whole procedure through which we would meet this living saint. And Emilio listened and then asked, 'Why do you want to meet her?'

"So I said, 'No, no, no! You don't understand. This will be a high point in our lives, meeting this extraordinary presence in the human race. We are blessed with the opportunity to meet this woman.'

"And Emilio said, 'Yeah, yeah, yeah, I understand all that. But why do YOU want to meet her?'

"I said, 'You're missing the whole point. We've got to meet this woman. It's very important.' And Emilio said again, 'But why do YOU want to meet her, Pop?'

"And finally I had to confess: I wanted to meet her so I could tell everyone I had. That was the only reason. So I didn't go. Emilio made me realize that I had already met Mother Theresa in spirit, and that she knew me.

"I believe we're all in this together, and nobody gets out

until we all get out. We cannot separate ourselves from each other."

And that was Martin Sheen in 1987, more than a decade before he became the television President many wish we could always have in the West Wing in real life: Forthright, humane, intelligent, articulate, and caring.

And by the way, Martin, I'm glad I didn't decide that I just wanted to meet you so I could tell everyone I had. I'm still glad I went to Toronto to meet you, because you were even more interesting than I thought you would be, and because you have grown more and more interesting as the years have gone by. A celebrity not afraid to speak his mind about issues he feels passionately about is a celebrity worth seeking out. In all my years of interviewing celebrities, you and John Wayne were the only ones who had the guts to speak out on sensitive political issues. And you, Mr. President — unlike ol' Duke, whose chapter I hope you'll read — were cold sober.

Chapter 12

JAMES EARL JONES: THE GREAT BLACK HOPE

The first time I ever heard the name of one of the great actors of our time, James Earl Jones, was in 1962, when the late Gladys Vaughan whispered a shortened version of it — Jimmy Jones — in my ear.

She had just arrived in Memphis to begin her stint as guest director of the Memphis Shakespeare Festival, of which I was a co-founder and board member. We had engaged her through the late Joe Papp, for whose New York Shakespeare Festival (Shakespeare-in-the-Park) she was a staff director.

Our contract called for her to stage the Festival production of "Much Ado About Nothing" at Memphis State University (now the University of Memphis). Vaughan, however, had a different idea, and couldn't wait to try to sell me on it. Because we were standing at a noisy club bar, she whispered her proposal in my ear: "Can we change the play? I want to do 'Othello' and I've got an actor in New York who's going to be a great Othello one of these days. His name is Jimmy Jones. We could bring him down and do 'Othello' here instead of 'Much Ado.'"

Without much ado, I told Vaughan that there was no way we could switch to "Othello." The University had yet to be integrated, and a year or so earlier, it had cancelled a scheduled production of "The Merchant of Venice" because of sensitivities about anti-semitism.

Two years later in New York, I got to see Jimmy Jones do what he called his first "real" Othello under Gladys Vaughan's direction. (He would do five more over the years.) Earlier that year at London's Old Vic, I had seen Laurence Olivier's stunning Othello, and here was a young African-American actor playing in the same league with England's greatest classical actor!

Four years after that, I met James Earl Jones for the first time, and saw him give one of the great bravura performances of our time in Howard Sackler's American tragedy, "The Great White Hope." Now I was convinced that Sidney Poitier had been right when he told me six months earlier that he believed James Earl Jones was likely to be the next black actor to become a major film star.

Two days after I saw his performance in "Great White Hope" at Broadway's Alvin Theatre, I met Jones backstage for an interview arranged by our mutual friend, Gladys Vaughan.

It was 5 o'clock on a gray Monday afternoon, and gentle Jimmy Jones seemed to have little connection with the fierce Jack Jefferson I had seen raging around the stage two

James Earl Jones, one of our greatest character actors. (Photo courtesy of James Earl Jones)

nights before. Jones's smile radiated its own warmth, without any help from the gold teeth he sported onstage. But the 6-foot, 1 1/2-inch form which seemed to expand to far greater size on the stage was huddled and withdrawn inside a terry-cloth robe at his dressing-table.

Even the rich, rolling voice was subdued by the residue of a cold, and the actor who inspired audiences to leap to their feet eight times a week to applaud and cheer confessed to feeling depressed by the physical condition in which he would soon have to climb that dramatic mountain again.

The play had premiered the year before at the Arena Stage in Washington, D.C. On Broadway it won the Pulitzer Prize, the Antoinette Perry Award, and the New York Drama Critics' Circle Award. Jones won the Tony for best actor, and Jane Alexander won it for best supporting actress. Both repeated their performances in the 1970 film version, which boosted both their careers.

In our backstage conversation, I learned that Jones had been born, and lived until age 6, in Tate County, Miss., near Arkabutla, 50 miles from Memphis. His grandparents raised him while his mother Ruth lived and worked in Memphis, and his father, Robert Earl Jones, looked for greener pastures elsewhere. "My parents are coming to the performance tonight," he confided with a frown. "That's always a trial. My father has seen the play several times, but my mother and stepfather are seeing it for the first time tonight. And with this cold I've got a damnable voice problem. I'm just beginning to be curious as to what's the best solution — for me to keep warming it up or try to let it rest. I don't know."

At the age of 6, Jones had lost his voice almost

completely. The trauma of being moved from his home in Arkabutla, first to Memphis with relatives he didn't know, then to the strange land of Michigan, where the grandparents he loved had moved to make a new home for the three of them, first caused him to stutter. Then the embarrassment of stuttering made him stop talking almost altogether. All this between the ages of 6 and 14.

During his first year in high school, he found his voice and cured his stutter under the wise and sympathetic tutelage of Donald E. Crouch, who taught English, Latin and history.

And what a voice he found! As Jack Jefferson, Othello, The Emperor Jones and Darth Vader, among others, his rich, reverberant voice has made theatres and TV sets rumble with rage, passion, power and authority.

In fact, in recent years, Jones's voice has become The Voice of Authority, endorsing products and services — especially as spokesperson for Verizon and CNN — so extensively that he is more often disembodied voice these days than the embodiment of some stage, screen, or TV character.

Many, including Sidney Poitier and myself, thought in the 1960s that James Earl Jones might be the black actor to challenge Poitier for African-American superstar honors. Instead, Jones became one of stage and screen's finest character actors.

In my 1968 interview, Jones had foreshadowed that choice when he told me he had come to the conclusion that all really fine actors were character actors. "I think that's the real stamp of a good actor, black or white. They're all character actors — Brando, Rod Steiger, Stacy Keach. Hollywood has kept trying to create another Clark Gable. They tried people like Rock Hudson and Tab Hunter, but they just didn't know what to do with types like Brando or Steiger.

"Or you," I suggested. "Watching you in 'Great White Hope,' and having seen you in 'Othello,' 'The Comedians,' and 'Dr. Strangelove,' I kept thinking that you're in that same category — an actor who can do such varied things and become so completely the character you're playing. In short: a character actor."

Today, at 70, Jones seems mainly content to work as a visible spokesperson, or simply as a voice of authority. Between news stories on television, I hear him intone: "THIS (pause) is CNN!" And every time I call my wife on her cell phone when she's not in the car, I hear Darth Vader intone: "WELCOME (pause) to Verizon Wireless!" Then some vocal nonentity adds: "The cellular customer you have called is not available at this time. . ."

As far as live theatre goes these days, Jimmy Jones doesn't seem to be available, either. But he has surely been one of the greatest, most versatile, and most adventurous character actors of our time.

As the late Alec Guinness might have said: May the Force be with him.

Chapter 13

THE NEWMANS: THE EYES, AND EYEBROWS, HAVE IT

Behind matinee idol Paul Newman's blue-blue eyes, there have always been a fine director and a terrific character actor, fighting to get out. He once said his epitaph would probably read: "He was a great actor — until his eyes turned brown."

In the course of the four interviews I have done with Newman over the years, I've had fascinating glimpses of the matinee idol, the character actor, and the director. And in two encounters 20 years apart, I have been charmed by the equally unaffected honesty of Joanne Woodward, the superb actress these three guys married.

One of the most revealing of my four interviews with Newman was done in connection with one of his least successful films, the 1976 release, "Buffalo Bill and the Indians," directed by Robert Altman. After Altman screened his preliminary cut of the film, Newman told our small group of film critics why he identified so closely with the film's protagonist, William F. (Buffalo Bill) Cody. One of the film's themes is that Cody deliberately buffaloed the public to create his own legend — and build audiences for his touring wild west shows.

"He was, symbolically, the first star — the first superstar if you want to call him that," Newman said earnestly. "A combination of General Custer, Clark Gable, Robert Redford and me — in that order.

"He was glamorized, and he became a legend he couldn't live up to, like the people in motion pictures who cannot live up to their legends. Their legends are created for them, and they are simply human beings."

How are the legends created?

"Just read any movie magazine, gossip column, or watch any entertainment show on TV — the quotes that simply were never said, the interviews that were never given, the conflicts, the joys — whatever it is you read about people that simply isn't true.

"The stuff I read about myself has absolutely nothing to do with me. And I must say it's a very humbling experience. All Cody was — all any of us so-called stars are — is a flawed human being."

As the interview wore on, Newman began to get a little carried away with his analysis of the film and its characters.

"To me," he said, "the picture is simply a canvas, and it has a lot of different colors in it. Some people may choose to linger on the reds, or think that the blues are important colors...."

At this point, Altman interrupted drily: "There's no blue in the picture, Paul."

Whereupon Newman, convulsed with laughter, explained: "Bob told me in the beginning that he was simply going to eliminate the color blue in the picture. The colors were going to be all warm tans and reds. I said, 'Well, I don't know' (covering his piercing blue orbs), 'I guess I'll have to play him blind.'"

The whole colloquy reminded me of a year earlier, when I was invited to attend a Lincoln Center Film Society gala honoring Newman and Woodward, and Paul told this story on himself: "I came in from an interview yesterday, and told Joanne: 'God! I'm so sick of the sound of my own voice!' And she said: 'Why were you listening to yourself?'"

That 1975 Lincoln Center Film Gala began with two hours and 20 minutes of excerpts from their films — his, hers, and theirs. When the curtains finally closed on the excerpts in the center's Avery Fisher Hall, Joanne rose to speak, and in her first sentence punctured any possible pomposity that might have been associated with the occasion.

"Um!" she grunted." "That was longer than 'Gone With the Wind'!"

It was the same honesty and lack of affectation — this cutting through to the essence of a situation or a character — that has distinguished the best of both actors' performances on the screen:

Her desperate but undeluded Beatrice Hunsdorfer in "The Effect of Gamma Rays on Man-in-the-Moon Marigolds," directed by Newman.

Her uninhibited Carol Cutrere in the roadhouse

"juking" scene from Tennessee Williams' "The Fugitive Kind," with Marlon Brando.

His detached yet electric presence opposite Elizabeth Taylor in Williams' "Cat on a Hot Tin Roof."

His conscienceless attempt at the verbal seduction of Patricia Neal's womanly wise (and Oscar-winning) housekeeper in "Hud."

His dead-on Rocky Graziano portrait in "Somebody Up There Likes Me." And their romantic-combative sparking of each other in sequences from "The Long Hot Summer," "From the Terrace," and "The Drowning Pool." After the film presentation, there was a black-tie party for donors to the New York Film Society in the lobbies of the New York State Theatre, across the court from the Avery Fisher Hall. A large table was reserved for the Newman/Woodward party, set off from the masses by encircling velvet ropes attached to brass standards, which were attended by a pair of important-looking security men. Shortly after the Newmans arrived and sat down at their tables, the standards and the velvet ropes were removed, obviously on Newman's orders, and the stars mingled freely with the masses.

Taking a seat by Joanne, I reminded her of our previous meeting in Hollywood almost 20 years before, when she was making her third film, "The Three Faces of Eve," which would win her the best-actress Oscar.

We had met over dinner in 1957 in the Crown Room of Romanoff's, the late, lamented, posh Hollywood restaurant where her studio, 20th Century-Fox, was entertaining the cast of newspaper critics and columnists working as extras in Paramount's "Teacher's Pet."

When we were introduced, she exclaimed: "From MEMPHIS? The PRESS-SCIMITAR! Why, I was in your Maid of Cotton contest there in 1949. I didn't win it, though, dog-gone it. And I sure wanted that trip to Europe."

Blond and impish, she confided to me that she had thought ever since that the reason she didn't win was the thought that flashed through her head when she first walked down the platform at Ellis Auditorium (razed in 1999 to make way for an arts center).

"I thought, it looks just like the runway in a burlesque house. Any minute, I expected a band to start playing 'A Pretty Girl Is Like a Melody.' And when I looked down at all those people in the audience, I just broke up — busted right out laughing."

The Maid of Cotton contest was co-sponsored by The Press-Scimitar and the National Cotton Council. Joanne represented Greenville, S.C., in the 1949 competition. When she failed to win the title, she had finished her drama major at Louisiana State University, then gone to New York to study at the Neighborhood Playhouse. Her first professional appearance was on the TV drama show, Robert Montgomery Presents.

"Since then," she told me with pardonable pride in 1957, "I haven't been out of work for more than two weeks at a stretch."

The "Three Faces of Eve" role had come as a pleasant surprise as she was preparing to return to Hollywood to appear in the film version of John Steinbeck's "The Wayward Bus." "My agent called," she said, and told me I wasn't going to do 'The Wayward Bus.' I had been picked to star in 'Three Faces of Eve.' I hadn't even tested for the part, or anything. In fact,

Joanne Woodward with the author in Hollywood in 1957, just before she zoomed to stardom, and her first Oscar, in "The Three Faces of Eve."
(Author's collection)

testing for me has always been like trying for the Maid of Cotton: I've never gotten a part I tested for."

Sitting at her table in the lobby of the New York State Theatre in 1975, I reminded her of our previous meeting in 1957, and that conversation we had had about the Maid of Cotton contest.

"I asked you if just being in the competition, even though you didn't win, had helped you toward your career goal," I said, "and I have always treasured your answer. Do you remember what it was?"

Her gray-green eyes sparkled as she recalled and repeated her 1957 response: "Well, Candy Jones was one of the judges, and she showed me how to pluck my eyebrows. If it hadn't been for the Maid of Cotton Contest, I would still have bushy eyebrows."

"Yes, and that's about all I did get out of it," she concluded above the rising hubbub of voices around her in the New York State Theatre. "Do they still have that contest? They do? Oh God, I ought to send one of my girls down and let her win it, which she would, and vindicate myself."

Though I have never had the opportunity to do a full-scale interview with Joanne, Paul has usually talked about her career in my interviews with him.

For example, all the women's roles in "Buffalo Bill and the Indians," even including Geraldine Chaplin's as Annie Oakley, were minor, so I asked Newman why there were so few good women's roles in films at that time. My question was clearly one that interested him.

"I have read a lot of scripts about women myself," he said. "They are almost exclusively about ladies in their 40s who are divorced and are trying to find a new way in life. Having more women writing screenplays might help. Like men's scripts, some would be bad, but some would be good and get produced."

Newman himself undertook from time to time to find good scripts for Joanne and direct them himself, in order to get them produced. When I asked which had been more gratifying for him — acting or directing — he said directing, without hesitation.

"I was a directing major at Yale Drama School. I never much desired to be an actor. It was Joanne who talked me into getting back to it."

I wondered if directing his wife had brought about any domestic strain, or if he and Joanne had been able to leave it behind when they left the set.

"Well," he admitted, "it caused plenty of strain in 'Gamma Rays.' That is the only time. It really did. Joanne has played marvelous, appealing, alluring, sexy characters in a lot of films, and she's only chosen to bring one of them home with her at night — and it had to be Beatrice Hunsdorfer. That's the only time in 20 years that she has brought a character home with her. And every time she brought Beatrice home, I left the house."

On two occasions I heard women columnists blame Newman himself for the shortage of good women's themes and roles in films. "You and Robert Redford started the whole buddy-buddy cycle with 'Butch Cassidy and the Sundance Kid,'" one declared.

"Oh hell!," Newman exploded. "What about Gable and Tracy?"

"But they," the lady rejoined, "always had Myrna Loy or Hedy Lamarr between them."

"Well," Newman shot back, "Katherine Ross ain't all that bad!"

On another occasion another female columnist asked Newman, apropos of nothing, apparently, except Newman's mesmerizing sex appeal: "Do you really want to go steady with Robert Redford?"

Said Paul: "Well, if he's willing.... Actually, we have marvelous hustles going back and forth all the time. For my birthday, he bought me a Porsche. He brought it in with a wrecker. He hit a telephone pole with it going about 90 miles an hour — sideways. It had no transmission, no clutch, no

The author and his wife at the New York press preview of "Buffalo Bill and the Indians." (Photo courtesy of Paul Schumach)

Paul Newman and the author's wife Tugar at the Atlanta premiere of "Fort Apache: The Bronx." (Author's collection)

seats, no wheels. That was my birthday. I had it compacted, and sent it back to him.

"I was really going to fix up his skis. He skis on Molnar 185s with Solomon bindings. I got a pair of them and was going to mount the bindings an inch and a half in FRONT of center. And they have these long ducts to give the skis torque. So you penetrate those little ducts, and half fill them with mercury so that every time the ski changes position, it relocates its balance.... Joanne talked me out of it, though."

A recurring theme in all my interviews with Newman — including sessions at the premieres of "Slap Shot" in 1977 and "Fort Apache, The Bronx" in 1981 — was his general aversion to interviews. Since we seemed to be getting along well in the one I conducted with him in Atlanta on "Fort Apache," I asked him why he disliked doing interviews.

Smiling wryly, he said, "All interviews tend to produce the same questions. A favorite question for me is, 'What's it like to work with your wife?' Having answered that question once, you are either forced to repeat the answer, which is likely to come out very boring, or to invent something that never existed so that you can feel fresh about it. In either case, you're the loser.

"I don't know what to add to that. I'm a private person for the most part. I wish I were something other than that. More like Muhammad Ali, for example.

"I remember once not too long ago, somebody — Burt Reynolds I think it was, who is not exactly a shrinking violet — was trying to smuggle himself off an airplane without attracting any attention. You know: you duck your head and stick matchbooks in your mouth and so forth. And so Muhammad saw Burt from way across the corridor and yelled out, 'Hey there, boy! Hey There, movie star! Why you creepin' around like that?' Of course, by that time Burt was trying to crawl back on the plane.

"I really wish I could be more like Muhammad, because he's so much happier in terms of the way he lives than I am.

"Or take the perfect example — Sophia Loren! Sophia making an entrance into a crowded restaurant is absolutely incredible.

"Joanne sneaks over to the hat-check girl and checks her coat, and we both try to slide into the restaurant sideways without being seen.

"But Sophia! She walks in, throws her shoulders back, her coat slides off and somebody catches it while she prances to her table.

"Holy Christ! I'd give a million dollars to be able to make an entrance like that."

So saying, Paul Newman made his goodbyes, slipped on his ever-present dark glasses, and set out as unobtrusively as possible across the lobby of the Atlanta Hilton.

The Newmans' reluctance to exploit their celebrity extends to their astounding record of sharing their good fortune with others. You won't hear it from them, but by 1998 (the last year for which I've found figures) his Newman's Own Foods, which began with his salad dressing recipe, had donated more than $100 million to his Hole-in-the-Wall Gangs, the Scott Newman Fund, memorializing his son, and other charities. The Hole-in-the-Wall Gangs (there were four of them the last I heard, named for the gang in "Butch Cassidy") are camps for sick kids, with hospital-standard medical facilities that allow even cancer and leukemia patients to take part. Paul Newman and Joanne Woodward, more than almost anybody I can think of, have given celebrity a good name. In addition to which, she has impeccable, non-bushy, eyebrows, and his eyes are still blue.

Chapter 14

PATRICIA NEAL IN THE VALLEY OF THE DAHLS

The Knoxville High School Class of '43 was holding its 30th anniversary reunion in the Mediterranean-style villa of Mr. and Mrs. H. Calvin Walter on Westland Drive.

It was in many respects like any other class reunion. Shouts of "Hey, ole buddy!" and "I bet you don't remember me!" punctuated the gossip and speculation about those who were, and were not, there.

Those who were there smiled a lot, and tried to look as prosperous and happy as they could.

But this Class of '43 had a special distinction, and this gathering in Knoxville, Tenn., was more than a reunion. It was also an homage, a tribute, to the tall, striking brunette who was clearly its center of attraction.

Her name was Patricia Neal, and this was her first visit

to her old home town since three massive strokes had felled her in 1965 at the peak of her acting career, destroying her memory and her ability to speak, and permanently impairing her eyesight and her mobility.

She stood at the head of the receiving line, just inside the front door of the Walters' house, greeting her former classmates as they arrived, and I, though not a member of the Class of '43, stood just behind her. (I had been a member of the Class of '42, but had moved to Memphis after just one year in Knoxville High School.)

I had known Patricia Neal — Patsy as we all called her then — since about 1937 when we were both students at Park Junior High School in Knoxville. She had given me my first, and only, nickname, Sarcy, for sarcastic, which I was not proud of, and was glad nobody else picked up.

I came back from World War II to discover that my old schoolmate Patsy was now known as Patricia Neal, and had quite a career going for herself on Broadway. In 1947, the first year the Antoinette Perry (Tony) Awards were given, she was named best supporting actress for her portrayal of the ruthless Regina in Lillian Hellman's "Another Part of the Forest," a prequel to "The Little Foxes," in which another Southern actress, Tallulah Bankhead, had also triumphed as Regina Hubbard 20 years further along in her evil conniving. (The Tony then was betokened not by a statuette, but, for the women, an engraved compact. A few years ago, at least, Pat still had hers, with the P.N. on it.)

Hollywood called, and in 1949 Pat toured to promote her first motion picture, a romantic comedy called "John Loves Mary," in which she co-starred with Ronald Reagan. By this

Touring to promote her first film, 1949's "John Loves Mary," co-starring Ronald Reagan, Patricia Neal is met at the train station in Memphis by the author. (Author's collection)

time, I was entertainment editor of The Memphis Press-Scimitar, and met her train at Memphis' Central Station to do my first interview with her as a celebrity. Warner Bros. was giving her the glamor treatment Hollywood laid on all talented young actresses in those days, so she arrived in Memphis wearing a swirling cape and a high-fashion equivalent of a Chinese coolie hat. Underneath the ultra-chic veneer, however, I discovered the old Patsy Neal, excitedly telling me that in her next picture as "PahTREESH-Ah," she would be co-starring with Gary Cooper.

Not long after the film — Ayn Rand's "The Fountainhead" — went into production, the Hollywood gossip columns were full of rumors that this new young star from Broadway was breaking up Cooper's marriage. Years later in Memphis during a 1976 interview with King Vidor, one of Hollywood's all-time greats, who had directed "The Fountainhead," I learned how quickly the romantic lightning had struck the two.

"They fell in love the first day," Vidor told me. "Pat rode up with me from Los Angeles to Fresno for the start of the picture. We had dinner with Coop the first night, a Sunday night, and you didn't have to be very alert to see them falling in love. That was about the last time I had the pleasure of having dinner with her. From then on she was with Coop every night. I liked them both — great people."

By the time I had lunch with Pat in 1951 on the 20th Century-Fox lot, where she was co-starring with Michael Rennie in a science-fiction film destined to become a cult classic, "The Day the Earth Stood Still" (which was NOT about the day she first saw Coop) the affair with Cooper was all over the papers, and she didn't want to talk about it. The actor's wife,

Rocky, had threatened to leave him. When Cooper came down with a severe attack of stomach ulcers, his mother called Pat and told her it was all her fault.

That was it for Pat; she told him she couldn't see him again. What she told me was that the whole thing was embarrassing and she'd rather not talk about it. She was uncharacteristically quiet and subdued all through lunch, until she told me about the toughest line she had ever been required to speak on stage or screen. The line, which she had to say quite seriously to a robot named Gort in the film she was making, was: "Klaatu barada nikto!"

"It took me half a dozen takes to get it right," she told me, laughing her infectious laugh for the first time that day, "because I couldn't say it with a straight face."

As soon as she could get out of her film commitments, the heart-broken Pat went to visit her sister in Atlanta, and stayed on for six months, licking her wounds. (I didn't know until I read her 1988 autobiography, "As I Am," that she had Cooper's child aborted and regretted it ever after.)

Then Pat went back to Broadway and starred in a revival of her friend Lillian Hellman's "The Children's Hour." At a party at Hellman's apartment just before rehearsals began, she met a handsome, dashing, 6-foot-6 young English writer named Roald (pronounced Roo-all) Dahl. The next time I saw her, in 1956, on Piggott, Ark., and Memphis locations for Budd Schulberg and Elia Kazan's "A Face in the Crowd," she had been married to Dahl for three years and they had a 1 1/2-year-old daughter named Olivia.

In Piggott Pat told me, "I get letters from Roald at our summer home in Great Missenden, England, telling me about

Pat Neal on location in Piggott, Ark., for Elia Kazan's 1957 film, "A Face In The Crowd." (Author's collection)

Olivia playing with dolls, and I can hardly bear not seeing her till they meet me in New York in November. But this was too wonderful a part to turn down. And Roald said I wouldn't be fit to live with for five years if I didn't take it."

The food in Piggott was so bad that at the end of my first day on location I was recruited by Pat and two of her co-stars — Andy Griffith, debuting on screen in the title role, and Anthony Franciosa, also in his first film outing — to drive them to nearby Kennett, Mo., for a real meal at the local hotel. During the drive, they all talked excitedly about the film and what a brilliant director "Gadge" (Kazan) was. He had discovered Pat doing a scene at the Actors Studio and cast her to substitute for Barbara Bel Geddes during her three-week vacation from his Broadway production of Tennessee Williams' "Cat on a Hot Tin Roof." He liked her work so much in it that he decided to star her as Marcia Jeffries, the small-town radio reporter who interviews Rhodes in the Picket, Ark., jail, is fascinated by his energy, dynamism, and folksy philosophizing, and sees her chance to ride his coattails to the big-time. But when he gets into political commentary, she gradually realizes she has created a monster. (This, of course, was long before Howard Stern or Rush Limbaugh was ever thought of.)

I didn't get to hear much from Pat in Arkansas about her new life as wife of Roald and mother of Olivia, but a few days later when the company moved to Memphis, my then wife (coincidentally also named Olivia) and our 1 1/2-year-old daughter Meg and I got to have Pat all to ourselves one evening for backyard barbecue. Although Meg and Pat were later to become friends in Los Angeles, their relationship did not get off to an auspicious beginning that August of 1956. I had Meg in her car-seat when I picked Pat up at the Claridge Hotel, and as we started out toward East Memphis, new mother Pat began entertaining Meg with an English nursery rhyme she said her own baby daughter Olivia loved.

"Round and round the garden," she began in that deep, rich, mahogony voice, meanwhile circling little Meg's stomach with her index finger, "like a Teddy Bear! . . .

"One step, two steps," lightly punching Meg's chest with each step, "and," chucking her under the chin, "TIDDLEY UNDER THERE!"

What was of course said playfully by Pat sounded, in her powerful, dramatic voice, ominous to little Meg. When Pat tiddleyed her, she burst into tears of fright, and whimpered intermittently all the way home. But it was a minor incident in a memorable evening, during which I got acquainted with a brand-new Pat Neal, relaxed, happy, and full of stories about her "delicious" baby Olivia, and her new life, spending summers in England and winters in New York so she could still do Broadway plays.

I didn't see Pat Neal again until that class reunion in Knoxville some 17 years later, but I kept up with her through correspondence and the media during the two major tragedies that struck her and husband Roald Dahl even before her debilitating strokes.

The first blow came in 1960.

It was Dec. 5, one of those bracing, sunny December days in New York City, just before the season's first big blizzard. Pat had just completed her role in "Breakfast at Tiffany's." Roald was in their apartment on the Upper East Side, writing one of his bizarre short stories. Little Olivia, now 5, was at kindergarten, and Pat had gone grocery shopping with 3-year-old Tessa, 4-month-old Theo, and their nanny, Susan Denson, who kept the two children outside in the sunshine while Pat was in the grocery.

As Pat tested the firmness of a grapefruit in the entrance to the store on Madison between 80th and 81st Sts., she could see Miss Denson wheeling Theo's carriage up toward 82nd St. with little Tessa toddling along behind.

A few minutes later, from farther back in the store, Pat heard a police siren and looked out the front window as the traffic patrol car sped by. But not until she had left the store and started up the street did she learn the awful significance of that siren.

With tears streaming down her face and a bewildered

Tessa in her arms, Miss Denson ran toward Pat, sobbing that Theo had been hit in his carriage by a taxi and was being rushed to the hospital by the police. The cab had run a red light at Madison and 82nd St. and knocked the baby carriage into a bus, critically injuring the Dahls' only son.

A week later, I was able to reach writer Dahl by telephone. We had never met, but when I told him I was an old friend of Pat's and a columnist in Memphis, he brought me up to date on Theo's condition. The infant had undergone a successful cranial operation the previous Saturday at Columbia Presbyterian Hospital Medical Center to relieve a blood clot caused by multiple skull fractures.

"They may have to operate again to relieve another clot," Dahl told me, "but meanwhile Theo seems to be coming through very well. At the moment, there are great hopes that everything is normal, but one can't be sure."

Sadly, everything was not normal, and in Knoxville, more than a dozen years later, Pat gave me more details.

"When Theo was injured," she said, "they sent him home from the hospital blind. We didn't realize that when he was hit, his eye went falling out. Roald discovered it when he put his face down right next to Theo's and he didn't even blink. But they were able to do an operation that restored his eyesight. He wears thick glasses now, you know. His balance isn't very good, and darling, he's always at the bottom of his class. But he's a delicious boy, and I love him."

Over the three years following the accident, Theo had to have eight more craniotomies to relieve his hydrocephalus, commonly called "water on the brain." It is a build-up of cerebro-spinal fluid that puts pressure on the brain. At that time, the technique of relieving it involved the insertion of a thin tube from the brain to a vein in the neck that would drain the fluid harmlessly into the bloodstream. The trouble was that the one-way valve in the tube kept clogging up. Each time it did, baby Theo would develop a fever and go blind again until he could be operated on to change the tube and the clogged valve.

Dahl decided there had to be a better way. As author Jeremy Treglown fascinatingly relates in his excellent and evenhanded "Roald Dahl: A Biography," he studied the problem in consultation with Theo's neurosurgeon Kenneth Till and his own friend Stanley Wade, who made tiny engines for model airplanes. In collaboration, they invented and patented the Wade-Dahl-Till Valve, which was exported all over the world and, before it was superseded, used successfully to treat between 2,000 and 3,000 children. But not Theo. Ironically, he had got better while his father was working on it, and no longer needed a shunt.

Two years later, tragedy had struck the Dahls again. They had moved from the dangerous streets of New York to the peaceful little Buckinghamshire village of Great Missenden. But the remorseless Furies that had seemed to pursue Pat through much of her life found them there and attacked again. Her "delicious" Olivia, aged 7, was suddenly stricken with measles encephalitis (it was not then the custom in England to inoculate against measles). They called the doctor, who said her heart was fine, her lungs were fine, and she'd be fine in a few days. She died before the night was over.

With all of that, plus the strokes she had suffered during the filming of John Ford's "Seven Women," strokes from which Roald almost literally called her back to life — slapping her cheeks, peeling her eyelids back, and shouting into her ear, "Pat! This is Roald! Pat! Tessa says hello! Theo says hello!", then organizing the rehabilitation that taught her to speak and walk again — it seemed almost incredible that now, eight years after the strokes, my old schoolmate could be standing here at her class reunion, nonchalantly greeting other members of the Knoxville High School Class of '43.

"Hi, Patsy!" they would say. "Bet you don't remember me!," and "Guess who I am, Patsy."

Grinning goodnaturedly, she would say, "Honey, I remember everybody! I remember everybody's face, but nobody's name. That's just the way I am. Who are you?"

Her memory had not been wiped clean like a child's magic slate, but it had been riddled with holes, and all the names and words had fallen through. (Twenty years later on a cruise to Tahiti during which we occupied adjoining staterooms on Cunard's Sagafjord, I was deeply moved to hear her tell how Theo had welcomed her "as a fellow student of the alphabet, taking over as soon as the speech therapist left the house. He would bring out his collection of flash cards, and together we would experience the joy of recognizing words like sister, orange, and trousers.")

Before wangling an assignment from my city editor in Memphis to go to Knoxville and cover Pat's return to our old home town, I had written her several letters in Great Missenden, reminding her who I was and telling her stories of our relationship — in school and later in Memphis, Arkansas and Hollywood. So when we had our own private reunion earlier that day at the home of her first dramatics teacher, Emily

Hahn (Mrs. Hugh Faust Jr.), she had known my name from my memory-jogging letters.

As Pat, Emily, my now 18-year-old daughter Meg and I sat reminiscing in the Fausts' garden, we talked, not about Pat's tragedies, but her beginnings and her triumphs.

At the age of 10 or 11, young Patsy had attended a performance by a woman giving monologues and acquired the ambition to do the same. As a Christmas present, her parents enrolled her with Knoxville's leading "expression" teacher, this same Emily Hahn, who had studied acting in New York, and who was her father's boss's sister, besides.

"Remember, Patsy?" she recalled, "I warned you, 'Your height will be a problem. You'll miss parts. You can never play ingenue roles, but you keep in the business till you're 30, and you'll have no problems.'"

Looking at her prize pupil sipping iced tea in the garden, she told me, "I think Patsy had her full growth when she first came to me at the age of 11. The thing I'm proudest of is that I took her and didn't ruin her. I let her do her own broad comedy. I didn't try to tone down her wonderful big voice, and I didn't try to tame her great zest and enthusiasm. I had her do monologues and cuttings before audiences all over town and watched her gain confidence and poise."

Said Pat: "I'm only 5-8, but I used to think I was the tallest person in the world."

I admitted that when we were kids, I had always been rather intimidated not only by Patsy's height, but by her poise, confidence, and commanding voice. She seemed so much more mature than the rest of our bunch. She was also witty, and at least as sarcastic as I was, which was why she recognized the trait in me and called me Sarcy.

Now, with a Tony in her purse and an Oscar on the shelf, she was recognized the world over as a great actress and a great lady after making a great comeback in "The Subject Was Roses" following her strokes. Having proved to Roald's satisfaction that she could do it, however — it was he, she told me, who was determined that she should act again — Pat was not very ambitious to keep at it. She felt she didn't do anything quite as well as she used to.

"I used to cook a lot," she said, "and made the beds, and cleaned the house, and all that sort of thing. But when I became ill, my husband started making a lot of money, and so we have all these people doing the work now, and it's impossible for me to do anything. Except that I dictate letters and I do the shopping — all the shopping.

"We have a lot of people come in for drinks before lunch, and drinks before supper, and for supper. Oh yes, and I am great at getting weeds out of the garden. That's what I do best."

Sitting there in that spring garden in Knoxville, to which Pat would return soon for the dedication of Fort Sanders Hospital's Patricia Neal Rehabilitation Center, her smile burst into bloom so often that it was hard to realize how many weeds had choked at her life since we had last met.

A little over two years later, in the fall of 1975, she greeted my new wife Tugar and me at the door of Gipsy House in Great Missenden. By the time she got the door open, we were surrounded by children, pets and visiting relatives in astonishing numbers.

There was Tessa, at 18 looking remarkably like her

mother had looked as a Knoxville schoolgirl; Ophelia, 11, looking a lot like Tessa; Lucy, 10 (who had survived Pat's strokes in her womb), a little shy and looking like herself; Roald's niece, Anna; her husband, Tom; their baby; the Dahls' Filipina housekeeper Evelyn, and two friendly dogs whose names I didn't quite catch. Roald and Theo, by now a fine-looking 6-footer of 15, were involved in Roald's weekly snooker ritual, but stuck their heads out of the billiard room to say hello.

Tugar and I had taken the train out from London and, following Pat's directions, walked through the quaintly charming little town to a narrow lane where we saw "Gipsy House" lettered on a wooden gate, and into the back garden past a ramshackle gypsy caravan.

Three more guests were coming out from London for dinner — Hiroshi Hayakawa, the son of Dahl's Japanese publisher; painter James Reeve, who was working on a portrait of Pat which would be a Christmas present for Roald; and Reeve's lady friend. But we had an hour with just Pat and Tessa before the next train, which would bring Hayakawa. Reeve was driving over and would take us all back to London so we wouldn't have to cut the evening short to catch the last train at 10:30.

When talking proved impossible in the breakfast room, which appeared to be the nerve center of Gipsy House, Pat took us into the sitting room which stepped down from the dining room and appeared to have been added on at some point. Indeed, the whole sprawling, whitewashed, old stone house gave the impression of having grown down the hillside it occupied as need, or whim, dictated.

All around the room were tables and desks of various

sizes, styles and periods, all united in comfortable confusion by their owners' eclectic tastes. The tables held various small stone, ceramic and metal sculptures, and the walls were covered with Picasso lithographs, a Constructivist painting or two, plaques and mementoes of both Pat's and Roald's careers. On a table behind the comfortably upholstered rocker in which Pat sat stood her Oscar for "Hud."

I told Tessa I had finally seen "Happy Mother's Day," the 1973-4 film in which she made her acting debut (and, as it happened, her swan song), when it had played on TV recently in the States, and thought she and her mother were both very good. In the ensuing conversation, I got the impression that, as a result of her long illness and rehabilitation, Pat had lost her parental role and become just one of the Dahl girls competing for Roald's approval, squabbling with Tessa and Ophelia rather than exerting any parental authority over them, or getting any parental respect.

There was a long diatribe, for example, between Pat and Tessa over the latter's announced intention to marry a young man named Dai Llewellyn, son of Col. Harry Llewellyn, who Tessa told us proudly was the only British equestrian to win a Gold Medal in the Helsinki Summer Olympics (in 1952). Again, Pat and Tessa were more like quarrelsome siblings than mother and daughter.

When Tessa first mentioned the young Llewellyn's name, Pat turned to me and said broadly:

PAT: "That is her fiance, she thinks."

TESSA: "What do you mean by that? You try that on me any more this weekend. . . !"

PAT: "Well, wait till you marry him to say you're going

to marry him. You don't know. . . ."

TESSA: "Well, as far as I know, we've arranged to get married . . . ."

(As things turned out, Tessa did not marry Llewellyn.)

I changed the subject to the London painter who was expected to arrive momentarily.

"His name is James Reeve," Pat said, "and he is now painting my portrait. Roald refused me permission to let James paint him, so I said, 'Would you like to paint me?' It's going to be Roald's Christmas present." Tessa volunteered that he was a very good painter, and very popular: "There's a six-page article in Vogue coming out on him." (Although Tessa's acting career had already begun and ended, she was, at 18, working as a model and frequently made the magazines and newspaper columns herself. She was often in the Cassini Carousel column and was one of Time magazine's "New Beauties" in a cover story the previous summer.)

Pat said of Reeve: "He's a lovely man. I adore him, and he paints so beautifully. For the picture, I am wearing this dress with spots on it — a green and brown dress with a V-neck that I bought in Florida — and over the dress (elaborate behind-the-hand stage whisper), I AM WEARING THAT MINK COAT THAT GARY COOPER GAVE ME. He's also going to put Roald's orchids in the painting, so he must get an orchid to take back with him tonight."

What neither Pat nor I had heard at the time were the rumors that Roald was having an affair with Felicity "Liccy" (pronounced Lissy) Crosland, the striking young advertising executive — mid-30s, recently divorced — assigned by the David Ogilvy agency to look after Pat during the years she was making a series of commercials for Maxim Coffee. I believe, however, that Tessa suspected this.

As Pat defiantly flung the Gary Cooper fur coat into the conversation, Tessa, looking conspiratorially toward my wife and me, asked her mother insinuatingly: "And uh, have you left the dress you wear in the painting at his flat?"

When Pat matter-of-factly said yes, Tessa said, "So you change there?" Pat, fully aware that Tessa enjoyed thinking that something was going on between her mother and James Reeve, laughed, "No. I don't even put it on."

"Well," said Tessa, continuing her captious tack, "there's definitely something going on, I think. . . ."

About that time, the gentleman in question made his entrance — a balding and effusive young man in a velvet jacket. When I inquired, he declared Pat to be a marvelous sitter: ". . . And she brings plastic buckets of delicious lentil soup, and one day she brought the most exquisite quiche. . . ."

Publisher Hayakawa, meanwhile, had arrived, and seemed a bit overwhelmed by the conversation, with Pat, Tessa, and Reeve and his lady friend, all talking at once. About this time, Roald came in, the snooker match being over, and announced that dinner was ready. We noticed that throughout the rest of the evening there was a combative, sort of chip-on-the-shoulder attitude between Pat and Roald.

Although Pat didn't learn positively of Roald's affair with Liccy, whom she thought of as her best friend, until later, I think she already sensed some important change in Roald that afternoon and evening we spent in Gipsy House. She mentioned several times during dinner that in Reeve's portrait she was wearing THE MINK COAT GARY COOPER GAVE ME, always looking mischievously at Roald for a reaction, a ploy which he pointedly ignored.

At table, Roald tyrannized Hayakawa all through dinner for allegedly driving a better car than his eight-year-old Rover, for staying at the Ritz, and for in general being richer than he, one of the authors on which Hayakawa and his father fattened. And when he tired of humiliating Hayakawa, he scolded Tessa for "lying in" and having a "daily" (maid) instead of getting up by 8 every morning, looking for modeling jobs, or "cleaning your own bloody house."

In spite of his rudeness, which I later learned was legendary (in Pat's autobiography, "As I Am," published in 1988, there are eight different page references in the index under "Roald's rudeness"), I found Dahl fascinating, and thought at the time we were hitting it off rather well.

For one thing, I admired tremendously the courage, fortitude and resourcefulness that enabled him to organize and insist upon the rehabilitation program he devised to give back to Pat a meaningful life instead of remaining a physical and mental cripple, as she might otherwise have been content to do. Also, I had read and reviewed his short story collections over the years — "Kiss Kiss," "Switch Bitch," and "Someone Like You" — and admired his writing style and his inventive, if often bizarre and morbid, plots. Of late, however, he had been writing more children's books and stories. (His 1964 "Charlie and the Chocolate Factory," later filmed as "Willy Wonka and the Chocolate Factory," had been a big success.) I was especially interested in hearing about his new children's novel, "Danny, the Champion of the World," which would go on sale in another week or two, and was to become one of his most successful books.

Halfway through dinner, I asked if he would mind my turning my tape recorder back on (it had been on before dinner, with Pat's approval), and asking him some questions about his writing. He agreed. A year or so later, when on a second visit to Great Missenden, where we had made other friends, Pat told me, "I'm sorry I can't have you at the house again. Roald is very angry at you." Pat wasn't sure why he was mad: "Something you wrote, I think." No doubt.

But what I wrote was simply what he had freely, indeed garrulously, told me about writing and publishing. "How do you shift gears," I asked, after he had shown me a copy of "Danny" hot off the press, "from adult stories to children's stories?"

"I don't know. You just shift, that's all," he said, seeming a little irritated at the question, as if it were perfectly obvious. Then he seemed to warm to the subject and gave me the following monologue on it:

"You've got to take about a month to shift. You've got to get into it, you know — into a child's world. I quite enjoy doing it. I used to enjoy adults very much — but children now. Lovely. You've got to live in an entirely different world.

"The mistake people make is that they think it's me, here, the ordinary chap, writing. But when you're working, you're a different fellow. For adult stories, you're using a certain part of you. For children's stories you're using another. It's nothing to do with who you are, sitting here. Different chap.

"Someone once said to Stravinsky, 'Maestro, where do you get your great ideas?' As if it might be in the bath, walking through the woods, or doing his teeth. And he made a very good answer. He said, 'At the piano.'

"At the piano! And we — we writers — do the same. We get it up there (tapping his high forehead), in the head. It's just the same. You get it when you sit down to work. You go to work, and out it comes. You don't get it walking through the bloody woods."

If I had cut off my tape recorder right there, at the end of his theme and variations on writing, perhaps Roald and I might have become friends. Instead, he switched from writing to publishing, and taxes, and I kept the tape recorder running.

Thinking back after reading Jeremy Treglown's 1994 biography of Dahl, I could see that it must have been the last two paragraphs of my December 1975 published interview that led him to tell Pat I was banned from the premises of Gipsy House.

"I am beginning to say to the publishers abroad, he told me at dinner, 'To hell with it,' because they are getting away with murder, and everything I get, the government takes, anyway. The biggest market is German. It's bigger than the English, you see — enormous, because the West Germans are big readers."

The former Royal Air Force wing commander, who had fought in the lost battle for Greece early in the war and been invalided to a desk job in Washington as assistant air attache at the British Embassy, went on: "I hate to say it, but they are exceptionally cultivated people, the Germans. There's a big strata there, and fine publishers, and they sell like hot cakes.

"But that's the one where I say I don't want any of their bloody money. It would only go to taxes if I got it. The sub-agent — we all have subagents, you know. I have an English agent who gets 10 per cent, and then there's 10 per cent for the German sub-agent. That's 20 per cent. So I said this German so-and-so (he actually said prick) can put it (Roald's German royalties) into Switzerland or somewhere. I don't want it. One's whole life now is to try to cheat these bloody income tax people."

When I read in Treglown that early in 1976 (a few months after our visit to Great Missenden and the interview I ran in December, 1975) Dahl had set up in Switzerland an "elaborate tax avoidance scheme" which he called Icarus S.A., I could easily imagine what Roald's reaction must have been as he read my interview, which I had sent to him by Pat when she and Theo visited Tugar and me in Memphis in January, 1976. (More about that in a minute.)

In the glow of the '64 St. Emilion and who knows how many pints consumed during the afternoon snooker match, he probably had not even realized that he had told me and my tape recorder how he contemplated "cheating these bloody income tax people."

If I had known he was dead serious, instead of just feeling put-upon like the rest of us, I probably wouldn't have printed the rancorous remarks about Switzerland and cheating. And even though I did, I think it very unlikely that any of those British income tax people ever read his remarks printed in a Memphis newspaper. Nevertheless, eventually the inland revenue did catch on to Roald and Icarus and, according to Treglown, bill him in the '80s for almost $1 million in overdue taxes.

Three months after our visit to what Tessa would later

call "the Valley of the Dahls" — a reference not only to the fact that members of her father's Norwegian family had proliferated through the Vale of Aylesbury since 1945, but also no doubt to her own and sister Lucy's troubles in the '70s and '80s — Patricia Neal and son Theo came to visit my wife Tugar and me in Memphis.

Perhaps the most gratifying part of the visit was the opportunity it gave us to discover what a fine young man Theo had become at 15. (He hadn't been able to get a word in edgewise during our chaotic visit to Great Missenden.) Pat and her 6-foot-2-inch son, who had suffered irreversible brain damage as an infant, were "doing the country" together, as she put it, after attending her niece's wedding in Atlanta. They had come to Memphis from our mutual home town, Knoxville, and were going on to visit other friends in Wichita, Kan., before

Visiting the Howards in Memphis in January, 1976, Neal and son Theo, then 15, are pictured with the author's wife Tugar. (Author's collection)

spending a week in Los Angeles.

She had entrusted their plane tickets to Theo, and would pointedly ask him questions about their flight number and departure time from Memphis, which he would answer with manly authority. He was solicitous about her: Was she tired, did she feel O.K.?

It was also my first chance to talk, uninterrupted, to Pat about the Dahl family tragedies, and how they had affected her philosophy of life, her thoughts about the future. After dinner, we all sat in the library in front of a cozy fire and I learned from Pat how the hammer-blows of grief and suffering had drawn her down a tortuous path first to extreme, almost fanatical, religiosity, then anger and non-belief, and finally to ironic acceptance of life — and death.

In the framework of a then current rash of IRA bombings in London and a recent bombing at LaGuardia Airport in New York, which she and Theo had passed through four days before, I asked Pat if her history of family tragedies made her worry more or less about her family's vulnerability to such events.

"No more than I always did — and no less," she said. "Life's very odd, you know. I'm fatalistic about it. I do think that what happens, happens, and it was meant to happen. I think.

"I think I've always been fatalistic, even though I was religious as a girl, you know. Very religious — until I went to Northwestern University. Then I found out a lot of my sorority sisters weren't religious — didn't believe in God — and I began to doubt.

"I wasn't religious again until I got married, and Theo

was run over   and damaged, weren't you, Tccdcc?," she said, reaching lovingly for her son's hand. "Then when, on top of that, our darling daughter Olivia caught the measles and died, I could hardly wait to join the church. I was very religious. I had been a Methodist as a child, and then when Olivia died I became a member of the Church of England."

Religion was a comfort for a while, she said. "But then," she recalled, "we were in California and I was starting to make 'Seven Women' for John Ford, and I had my strokes. When I finally woke up, I woke up not believing in anything. I think I was angry. I must have been very, very angry, because it lasted for several years."

Was she still angry?

"Yes, I am. I am very angry with Him," she said, looking heavenward and laughing an ironic laugh, and then amending, with another upward glance, "No, I'm not. Not really angry." She said she thought she still had some religious feeling, though she was no longer active in the church.

"Not one bit," she said positively. "The children have been once or twice to the Baptist Church in Great Missenden, but we don't have a Sunday School in the Church of England, which is in Little Missenden. I never go to church any more."

Although I knew Pat's strokes had wiped out that portion of her memory that stored names and other words, I had never been sure — even after reading Barry Farrell's definitive 1969 book, "Pat and Roald" — about her memory of events that occurred before her strokes. As the fire burned lower in the fireplace, I asked.

"Oh," she said, "I still can't remember names, and that sort of thing. But I still remember everything that happened.

But words are difficult. I'm still learning them. And physically — I walk with a little limp, and I don't use the pen well. But otherwise (and here she broke into one of her inimitable, boisterous, ironic, self-deprecating laughs), I'm perfectly normal."

The last embers of the fire were dying as I sent her off to bed with a book. She'd asked for one because she wasn't over her jet lag and was afraid she might have trouble sleeping. From my stock of books sent to me for review, I picked out "Radie's World," by then Hollywood Reporter columnist Radie Harris, which had just been published and included a chapter on Pat and Roald.

Next morning at breakfast, she gave Radie, an old acquaintance, high marks for friendliness and courage (she had had an artificial leg since an amputation at the age of 14), but not very high marks for accuracy.

Of Pat's love affair with Gary Cooper, for example, Harris wrote: "The two fell deeply in love, but Gary's wife, a devout Catholic, wouldn't listen to Gary's plea for a divorce."

Shaking her head, Pat said: "He never asked for one. Never. I assure you he did not. This is imagination."

She showed me another passage — "She (Pat) had grown quite heavy" — and corrected: "I weighed 115. I was skinny. You couldn't believe it. I lost masses and masses of weight, so that's ridiculous."

But the passage in the book that drew the biggest laugh from Pat was this one: "Roald was a helluva guy. He married Pat knowing she didn't love him." Chuckling and shaking her head, Pat told me: "The thought would never have occurred to Roald.

The question simply wouldn't have entered his head." Then, after a momentary pause, she added: "He's never even told me he loves me. My husband just doesn't say things like that."

Just before we loaded Pat and Theo and their luggage into our car for the trip to the airport, Pat handed me a lovely 8x10 color photograph of James Reeve's portrait of her wearing THAT MINK COAT GARY COOPER GAVE ME. Inscribed on the back was the following:

"To My Darlings — Tugar and Edwin — Until we meet again! Patricia Neal, January 3, 1976, Saturday."

Pat and Roald were finally divorced in 1983. Pat moved into a house on Martha's Vineyard and an apartment in New York City. We exchanged notes a couple of times.

Then in 1993, we met again on the Cunard Line's MS Sagafjord on a Theatre-at-Sea cruise from Los Angeles to Hawaii, Bora-Bora and Tahiti. On the ship, our stateroom was right next to that of Pat and her traveling companion. Tugar and I had got ourselves on this particular cruise for several reasons: I had dreamed of going to Tahiti since I first saw "Mutiny on the Bounty" at the Tennessee Theatre in Knoxville in 1935 (about two years before Pat and I became friends). And we thought it would be fun to have reunions aboardship with Pat and two other actor friends scheduled to make the trip — Dana Ivey and George Hearn. Hearn canceled at the last moment, but we loved sailing with Pat and Dana and Brian Bedford, Donna McKechnie, Richard Kiley and others who put on shows for us every evening at sea.

Pat still can't remember lines well enough to do plays, but I was moved by her dramatic reading of the inspirational autobiographical lecture Roald first wrote for her about 1968, revised versions of which she has been delivering ever since, and by her narration and singing in a Noel Coward revue one night. In a way, she was back where she started at 11, delivering monologues.

Roald had died in 1990, a few months after Pat had returned to Gipsy House for Theo's 30th birthday and a reconciliation, sought by her, with Roald and Liccy. "Having made our peace at least helped me cope with his passing," she movingly declared.

In all the years I have known her, I had never known Patricia Neal could sing, but on the Sagafjord one night as we neared Bora-Bora, I discovered there was music as well as drama in that big rich voice. In a single spotlight, with the lyrics on a lectern in front of her, Pat talk-sang these sadly jaunty Coward lines:

When the storm clouds are riding
Through a distant sky,
Sail away, sail away.
When the love light is fading
In your sweetheart's eyes,
Sail away, sail away . . . .
When the wind and the weather
Blow your dreams sky high,
Sail away, sail away, sail away.

☆ ☆ ☆

I don't mind telling you, she blew me away.

As I write this, I have beside me on my desk a photograph I took of Pat on the deck of the Sagafjord one day.

There's a rainbow 'round Neal's shoulder on the deck of the Vistafjord during the cruise. (Author's collection)

She is wearing a white terry-cloth robe and looking intently into the camera lens.

You can see on her face the lines etched there by the serial tragedies that have tracked her like scouts from hell. I had noticed during our two weeks together that she seemed to have forgotten how to laugh that great hearty laugh, but in the photograph, a gentle smile lifts the corners of her lips. And, close enough to cuddle her in its arched embrace, there's a rainbow 'round her shoulder.

Chapter 15

INGRID BERGMAN: THE FACE SHE EARNED

Headline, 1982: Ingrid Bergman Dies at 67.

Somehow, both pieces of information in that headline seemed impossible — that she was dead, and that she could have been 67. O.K., so she looked her age in her last performance, as Golde Meir on TV earlier that year. But the wrinkles, I was sure, were all make-up.

Perhaps there had been a few wrinkles the last time I had seen her, five years earlier in the lobby of the Vaudeville Theatre in London. But what I still saw was the perfect, unmade-up complexion and the flashing eyes that had captivated me the first time I met her, in a pyramidal tent in Italy just after World War II ended in 1945.

She and Jack Benny and harmonica virtuoso Larry Adler had just done a USO show for the U.S. 1st Armored Division.

Now Benny was glumly telling me, as editor of my division newspaper, "The Warrior," how tired he was, how he hadn't had a day off in weeks, and other grumbling complaints. Bergman listened to Benny for a few minutes, and then, with a radiant smile, punctuated by a peal of laughter, declared, "Why, Jack, you know we only did one show yesterday, and had the whole day off the day before!" That may have been the moment when Benny's slow burn, soon to be immortalized on television, was born.

Thirty-two years later in the lobby of the London theatre to which we had both come to see Glenda Jackson in Hugh Whitemore's moving play, "Stevie" (about the English poetess Stevie Smith), Miss Bergman was accompanied by her longtime friend and dialogue coach, Ruth Roberts. I reminded them of our days together in 1969 in Gatlinburg, Tenn., and environs, when the actress was co-starring with Anthony Quinn in Rachel Maddux's "A Walk in the Spring Rain."

By the time of this, our last encounter in London in 1977, all three of her marriages — to Dr. Peter Lindstrom, director Roberto Rosselini, and theatrical producer Lars Schmidt — had ended. Miss Bergman's world, which had included wide-ranging stage and film stardom and awards, houses at Choisel outside Paris and the Swedish coastal island of Dannholm, had narrowed to a modest apartment in Cheyne Walk in London. She had already had one mastectomy and would have to have another the next year in a bout with cancer that would finally bring her death.

But, recalling the Great Smoky Mountains of East Tennessee in that London theatre lobby, her face brightened.

"You know," she said in that inimitable husky voice with the barely perceptible, yet charming, accent: "Ruth and I were just talking about that. Do you know — it seems impossible — but it has been eight years this month since we went to the mountains to make that film."

She had loved the Smokies — Cade's Cove and Greenbrier Cove, especially, and the great outdoors in general. One night, walking back from dinner at Gatlinburg's Brass Lantern restaurant to her rooms at the River Terrace Motel, she listened raptly to author Rachel Maddux talk about the whippoorwill's song as the first sign of spring. "I live very close to nature, too," Bergman told us. "On Dannholm, our island, we live in a big wood house right on the sea. I have breakfast outside every morning. The seagulls come right up to the porch, and I throw bread to them. Oh, how I love my gulls! In the house, we used to have only candles, but we put in electricity five years ago to keep guests from burning the house down. I liked it better with the candles."

In her River Terrace suite, we talked on into the night. Among other things, I learned that "Casablanca," the film in which she captured the world's heart forever, was not her favorite.

"'Casablanca' was an impossible film to make," she declared. "The writers were on the set every day, making up the story as we went along. I didn't even know whether I was supposed to be in love with Bogart or Paul Henreid. They would say, 'Well, we aren't sure yet. Play it in between.' Finally I said, 'Which one do I go with at the end?' And they said, 'We don't know yet. We'll shoot it both ways.' And it's literally true that they didn't know which way it would end until they saw it

— after our director Michael Curtiz, had chosen between the two endings. And THEY won an Oscar!" (1943 was not a good year for Bergman. Besides not winning anything for her luminous guessing-game performance in "Casablanca," the best actress Oscar that year went to Jennifer Jones for "The Song of Bernadette," and Katina Paxinou won the best supporting actress award in Bergman's film, "For Whom the Bell Tolls.")

Earlier that day, up in Greenbrier Cove, one of my favorite Smoky Mountain haunts, I had been impressed by how easily co-star Anthony Quinn had swept Bergman up into his arms and carried her on stepping-stones across the Greenbrier Prong of the Little Pigeon River. Back at the River Terrace, I told the actress how much I liked the scene.

Eyes sparkling mischievously, she said, "There is a story behind that scene. When I made 'Dr. Jekyll and Mr. Hyde' with Spencer Tracy early in my career, there was a scene in which Spencer had to pick me up and carry me upstairs. Spencer was not a large man, and I am not a small woman. He took one look at the script and then at me, and said, 'Never! I couldn't do it in a million years.'

"So they rigged up a sling suspended from the ceiling and put me in it. Spencer stood next to me and put his arms around me, and in close-up it looked exactly as if he were carrying me.

"Well, the first time we did it, the man on the catwalk operating the sling went too fast, and there I was sailing up the stairs and poor Spencer running like mad to keep up. The next time we tried it, the sling slipped and I toppled down with him. It was a wonder we didn't break our necks. By this time, we were all so convulsed that it took several more takes to get it right.

We finally got it, but I resolved then and there never to be carried in a movie again.

"Now, there was this scene today that called for Tony to carry me across a little stream to get to some watercress. When I saw the script, I said, 'No. Give me some stepping-stones, or I'll wade across — anything,' and Stirling Silliphant changed the script.

"But later, when we came to the scene in a script run-through, Tony read the scene and said, 'Why don't I carry her?' I explained why, but he simply put down the script, scooped me up and said, 'No problem.' And I must say I felt very comfortable, very safe."

By that time a grandmother herself, like the character she played in the film, Bergman perhaps felt that it was no longer necessary always to keep both feet on the ground.

I also wanted to know more about Miss Roberts, and here's what she told me that night in Gatlinburg: "Yes, I was with Ingrid on her first American film, 'Intermezzo,' and I've been with her on most of them since. I was also dialogue coach for Loretta Young when she won an Oscar for playing a Swede in 'The Farmer's Daughter.' The Hollywood joke was that in 'Intermezzo' I took Ingrid's accent away and then gave it to Loretta in 'The Farmer's Daughter.'"

Earlier in 1969, I had interviewed Miss Bergman in Hollywood, to which she had just returned after 20 years of exile. For the first time since running off to the Italian island of Stromboli with Italian director Roberto Rossellini in 1949, she was back in Movietown to co-star with Walter Matthau in the film version of the Broadway comedy hit, "Cactus Flower."

At a Hollywood Foreign Press Association luncheon in

the Beverly Hills Hotel, for which I had, you might say, obtained a visa from a studio press-agent friend, Bergman told me she had left Hollywood as much for artistic freedom as anything else.

"I was always tied up with a studio," she said, "and had to do whatever they wanted me to do instead of more

The author interviews Ingrid Bergman in the Beverly Hills Hotel in Los Angeles on her return to the U.S. to make "Cactus Flower," her first Hollywood film in 20 years. (Author's collection)

interesting things I might want to do. You felt, you know, like a horse in a stable. They took you out to ride you when they felt like it, then put you back in the stable.

"Also, 20 years ago, everyone made movies right here in the studios. I was the one who started to say, couldn't we, when we do 'Casablanca,' couldn't we go to Casablanca? When we do 'Notorious,' set in Brazil, couldn't we go to Brazil? And they said, 'No, it will be lovely on the back lot. Much better on the back lot.'

"So that's why I left. I didn't want to stay behind these walls. Now, 20 years later, it isn't like that anymore. Today they say, sign a contract with 20th Century-Fox and see the world. 'A Walk in the Spring Rain,' which I will do later this year for Stirling Silliphant, is set in Tennessee, and we will go to the mountains of Tennessee to film it."

Leaving her husband, Peter Lindstrom, to go with Rossellini had also meant leaving her daughter, Pia, but by 1969, Bergman told me she and Pia were reconciled, and her children by both Lindstrom and Rossellini were friends.

"The children are always happy to come to the island in Sweden," she told me. "Pia has spent a lot of time with me in Europe, and now she is a TV reporter in San Francisco. She comes down to visit me here in Hollywood and to film the Liars' Club game show, which is shown here. So before I go to bed I look at her at 11 o'clock on television. It's very nice."

In one of her last films, Ingmar Bergman's "Autumn Sonata" (1978), the actress would finally work through what had been one of the great conflicts in her own life — the desire to be with her children and the need to be free for her career.

I was always as impressed by Bergman's naturalness and

honesty as I was by her great beauty, charm and talent. The honesty was there from that first meeting in Italy when she confounded Jack Benny with it right up to her 67th year, when to Death's knock I think she must have replied matter-of-factly: "Yes, I've been expecting you. I am ready to go."

Chapter 16

WILLIAM HOLDEN: FOLLOWING THE SUN

My favorite memory of William Holden is the reply he gave me at the end of our last interview when I thanked him for what I still think were the best of his many films: "Sunset Boulevard," "Stalag 17," "Bridge on the River Kwai," and "Network." Grinning like Sefton in "Stalag 17," he said, "Yeah, but I bet you never saw 'Wild Girls of the Road,' 'Good Old Siwash,' 'Out of the Frying Pan,' or 'Those Were the Days.' I made pictures they took out of the studio at night because they were ashamed to ship them by daylight."

He was always irreverent about movies in general, and his own in particular.

The first time Holden and I came face to face was on the "Fort Bravo" set at MGM in 1953. The MGM lot was bustling that spring. The first 3-D feature, "Bwana Devil," had been released a few months before, and everybody was speculating on the clumsy device's future.

Fred Quimby, head of the studio's shorts department, told me: "'Tom and Jerry' are keeping abreast of the times. We're making at least one cartoon in 3-D."

On Stage 1, I watched a 17-year-old violin prodigy named Michael Rabin recording the violin track actor Vittorio Gassmann would appear to be playing in "Rhapsody," co-starring Elizabeth Taylor. No three-dimensional process for this film; the curvaceous Miss Taylor was considered 3-D enough.

But on Stage 29, Howard Keel was lip-synching a song for a sequence in Cole Porter's "Kiss Me, Kate," which the studio was filming in 3-D.

On an adjacent sound stage, I found Holden lounging around an interior setting for the Civil War Western, "Fort Bravo." He told me about a gag he wanted written into the picture. To illustrate, he walked over to a table on which sat an old-fashioned stereoscope, an antique device that made still photographs stand out in three dimensions.

The gag, he said, would be to have him walk over, pick it up, and ask, "What's this?"

"Then," he grinned, "somebody says, 'Oh, that's a stereoscope, a newfangled thing that makes pictures look three-dimensional.'"

Finally, illustrating the punchline, Holden raised the viewer to his eyes, peered meditatively at the twin pictures merged by it, put it back on the table, shook his head and said, "It'll never last."

And of course it didn't — 3-D, that is. It was a passing fancy for Hollywood, which decided that the screen should go wide with CinemaScope rather than deep with 3-D. But Holden sure lasted. He had already done at least four of the films that made major stardom a certainty for him — none of them in 3-D. They were "Sunset Boulevard," "Born Yesterday," "Stalag 17," and "Miss Grant Takes Richmond." And he was just getting started.

Although the least-known of that quartet, "Miss Grant Takes Richmond," which preceded the other three films, pointed the way to two spectacular careers — Holden's in comedy, and Lucille Ball's in television.

When I interviewed the irrepressible Lucy on the set of "Mame" in 1973, I told her it seemed to me that "Miss Grant" had contained the seeds of her first TV character, Lucy Ricardo.

"You're right," she smiled, "When I made up my mind to go into television, that was the film I chose as a kind of model." (See Chapter 5: "Lucille Ball: One Legend Who Loved It.") She said she wanted Holden to do another comedy with her years ago. "He was so good at comedy," she said, "but those long locations far away have been his wont for many years, and for many reasons."

I interviewed Holden four more times in the two decades following our first meeting on the "Fort Bravo" set as the wanderlust Lucy had noted led him to follow the sun to ever more remote locations around the world.

In Stockholm, Sweden, in October, 1960, he and Paramount's "The Counterfeit Traitor" company couldn't even find the sun, though, much less follow it.

He hadn't had a day off since starting "The World of Suzie Wong" the previous January in Hong Kong. "Traitor" had been plagued by weather problems and was two weeks behind schedule. There was no chance of his keeping an appointment in London on Oct.17.

In fact, on Oct.22, he, producer Bill Perlberg, and Erick Ericson, the big Swede whose real-life wartime espionage exploits Holden was portraying in the film, were still whiling away the days with 57 varieties of herring in the smorgasbord of the Grand Hotel, separating lunch from dinner with brandy, chocolates and cigars, and waiting for the sun to come out.

I was there with them, not caring if the sun ever came out, but I could see why Holden got a little testy on an indoor shot director George Seaton had improvised in a corridor of the hotel from one that had been written to be shot outside.

German actor Carl Bradley, playing an American OSS agent code-named "Memphis," had to be flown in from Berlin where he was rehearsing a new play. All day the "Traitor" company waited for him to arrive, and when he did, they found he had dyed his naturally blond hair black. It took two more hours of make-up magic, with greasepaint and powder, to make him look blond again. It took several takes to get the shot, and then the unit still photographer moved in, and you could hear Holden's patience crack all up and down the corridor.

"Stills!" he bellowed. "Why don't you use some 'Suzie Wong' stills. I wore the same suit!"

Director Seaton was watching the scene with an air of amused indulgence. A gentle, witty man, he smilingly retorted: "Then how come you sent us a bill for it?"

Holden cracked up, laughing. The tension was broken, and he was a good guy again. The still man got his stills.

Holden even threw in some fancy poses — a tour jeté, and a cloak-and-dagger crouch — that I'm sure are collectors' items now.

At 6:30 the next morning, though, Holden was down again. As I rode with him in a company limousine to Uppsala, north of Stockholm, for an outdoor scene predicated on a weather prediction of sunny skies that never came, he complained that his wife, the former actress Brenda Marshall, whom he called by her given name of Ardis, had kept him awake till 4 a.m., discussing college plans for their two sons.

"Dammit!" he exclaimed. "We could have discussed those things any time during the last three months Ardis has been on location with me. But she's leaving today (for their home in Switzerland), so she had to wait till her last night here to talk about it — and me with this 7:30 call in Uppsala!" Then with a shrug and a grin he concluded: "Oh well, that's the story of my wife."

I had met Mrs. Holden on the "Horse Soldiers" location in Natchitoches, La., two years before and found her as beautiful and charming as she had been on the screen before giving up her career to raise their two sons. But when their 29-year marriage ended in 1970, I dug out the two photos I had made of them having lunch on the Louisiana location. In one both were smiling lovingly at each other. In the other, apparently taken before they were ready, both looked ineffably sad. Had the smiling pose been just a pose? I wondered.

We always seemed to be eating when I was with Holden. In Natchitoches in 1958, it was franks and beans from paper plates as we leaned against his dressingroom/trailer on

William Holden with his wife Ardis, the actress known professionally as Brenda Marshall, on the "Horse Soldiers" location in Natchitoches, La., in 1959. (Author's collection)

a rutted road by the Cane River. Two years later in Stockholm it was luscious Swedish delicacies from the Grand Hotel smorgasbord, followed ceremoniously by cognac, chocolates and cigars.

Sixteen years after that, my wife Tugar and I were sitting in the Office Pub on 55th St. in New York during the lunch break from filming for Paddy Chayefsky's masterpiece, "Network". Lunching with us were the film's producer, Howard Gottfried, and Holden, who was in a reminiscent mood. I mentioned how well the morning's scenes had gone, with Chayefsky prowling the set, ready to make any script changes director Sidney Lumet might suggest. Holden, spooning chili over his scrambled eggs, and sour cream over his chili, agreed, and said "Network" reminded him of his 1954

MGM film, "Executive Suite."

"It was a good picture, too," he said, "innovative for its time. John Houseman was the producer, Bobby (Robert) Wise the director, and what a cast: Barbara Stanwyck, Nina Foch, Fredric March, Louis Calhern, Paul Douglas, Shelley Winters, June Allyson...."

"And we shot it in very short order, for $1 million. It was a fun film to work in because everybody was on his toes. I looked down that boardroom table and, as I panned around, there was Freddie March — he was my opposition in the corporation — Barbara, Louis, and Walter Pidgeon. I thought, 'No el Flubbo today!'

"It's been kind of like that on 'Network,' too. With Peter Finch, Bob Duvall, Faye Dunaway, and all these New York actors, we're all going into the bathroom at night to study our lines and make sure we're letter-perfect the next day."

At this point, my wife slipped in a question about her favorite Holden film, "Love Is a Many-Splendored Thing." How did it rank with him, or something like that.

"Funny you should mention that," he said. "I spent the afternoon with Han Su-Yin (author of the book on which the film was based) just the other day. She's here in New York to lecture somewhere Saturday. She lives in Lausanne, Switzerland, now. But I seem to see her almost everywhere but there. I used to go to Singapore and see her. I would see her in London, Hong Kong."

I hadn't asked him about Stephanie Powers, who we knew from the gossip columns had been his constant companion for a couple of years or more, but at this point he brought her into the conversation.

The author's wife Tugar with "Network" co-stars William Holden (left) and Peter Finch. Both were nominated for Oscars, and Finch won posthumously. (Photo courtesy of Paul Schumach)

"I took Steph over to meet her. She (Miss Su-Yin) is about 65 now, but God! What a woman! She's so damned bright! And so nice.

"Funny thing happened. She wouldn't go to see 'Love Is a Many-Splendored Thing' when it came out, because I wasn't an Englishman (as the character he played was), I think. She also saw Audrey Hepburn, whom I had suggested, as herself in the picture, much more than Jennifer Jones, who of course played her. So between that, and me, she never went to see the picture.

"Then about four years after the film was released — about 1960 — I was having dinner with her and the producer Run Run Shaw in Hong Kong, and he said to her, 'How did you like Bill as Morrison?' She said she didn't see me, and he said, 'You never saw "Love Is a Many-Splendored Thing?" Well, I have a print of it and you're going to see it right now.' She said, 'I'd rather not.' He insisted. I said, 'Don't embarrass the woman, Run Run,' but he persisted and she finally gave in.

"I wasn't about to watch it with her, and I didn't find out what happened until later. What happened was that she went back to the President Hotel in Kowloon and cried for two days. She is a helluva dame."

Acting was by this time the means to an end for Holden. Since our fruitless search for the sun in Sweden a decade and a half before, he had followed the sun into a new life. He had turned his Safari Club in Kenya (only recently purchased in 1960) from a hunt club into a game preserve. And now the sun that had bronzed his features in the intervening years shone on him not only in Africa, but in such exotic places as New Guinea and Yucatan, to which he regularly ventured on expeditions aimed at preserving endangered species of animals and birds.

When he finished "Network," he said, he would be going to the Bismarck Archipelago, northeast of New Guinea. Together with Jean-Michel Cousteau, Jacques' son, he would be translocating rare species of pigeon, dove, and bird of paradise to islands that could support them. "There are these other islands," he explained, "which have their own rain forests and can support bird life. I got involved with it a few years ago and go down there every year."

The next, and last time, I talked with Holden — in Dallas in June, 1978, for a regional premiere of "Damien — Omen II" — he was more interested in talking about his travels than the film. He was in Dallas to promote the film —

and he had outrun the sun, on the supersonic Concorde, to get there from the Cannes Film Festival — but he was too honest to lie about it.

"Working in a film like 'Network,'" he said, "you get emotionally involved with a fairly high level of creative artistry on the part of people like (writer) Paddy Chayefsky and (director) Sidney Lumet. There's an excitement about working in a film like that which isn't evident when you're just doing a sort of a job making a film.

"That's the difficulty of doing a film like 'Omen II.' Any time that excitement is lacking, it's a little more difficult to do a good job. You know what I mean? You haven't got that stimulation every day that makes you want to get in there and do something along with a bunch of people who are at the same time excited about it."

Getting "Damien II" out of the way as quickly as possible, Holden brought us up to date on his travels.

"Steph and I had quite a year this last year," he enthused. "We started down in Greece, then she went to Poland, to Warsaw, for this cultural exchange program (her real name is Stephanie Federkiewicz).

"I went to Germany to do 'Fedora' for Billy Wilder. Stephanie came back and made a movie for television, then flew to Germany and we spent time together there.

"From Germany, we moved to Paris, and Billy very kindly arranged the shooting schedule so Steph and I could get down to a game catch in Africa. We translocated some Grevy zebra from the northern frontier district, where they are endangered, down into game parks in southern Kenya.

"Then we went back to Paris and finished 'Fedora,' and

as we were finishing, the visas for China that we had been waiting a year and a half for came through, so we flew to L.A., changed clothes, re-packed, flew to Tokyo, and went into China for 11 days — Shanghai, Beijing and Canton."

Miss Powers had opened an art gallery in L.A., he said, and they had bought "a fair amount of art in China."

The relationship continued for several more years, then quietly ended, perhaps because of Holden's drinking problem. In November, 1981, we were shocked to learn that, drinking alone, he had fallen, cracked his head and bled to death.

Though he died alone — and probably because he was alone — William Holden was not a loner. He was friendly and gregarious. He loved being with people and talking about his vocation, and his avocation, which was nothing less than trying to save the planet's endangered species.

Even his closest friends failed to realize, until it was too late, that he, too, was an endangered species. We can only hope that in his last moments, he saw his way through to whatever destination he had been so avidly seeking for so many years.

Chapter 17

JACK NICHOLSON: JUST ACTING CRAZY

The eyes of Jack Nicholson are a gold-flecked green, slumbrous and enigmatic — cat eyes. His smile is self-satisfied, all-knowing, and almost ever-present. The combination suggests nothing so much as the Cheshire Cat. And, just like the Duchess's grinning feline pet in "Alice in Wonderland," he has, during an interview, a disconcerting habit of gradually fading away from it, only to re-enter the exchange just as gradually, or all at once, or perhaps to vanish from the conversation altogether.

Such evanescence may be partially, but not entirely, willful. During an interview with a press group, including myself, on the occasion of the world premiere of "One Flew Over the Cuckoo's Nest" in New York City in 1975, the actor explained his feelings about interviews:

*At the premiere of "One Flew Over The Cuckoo's Nest" in New York in
1975, the author's wife gets an autographed photograph from Jack Nicholson.*
(Photo courtesy of Paul Schumach)

"You all know that there are many different techniques
of being interviewed. Short answers for some people, long for
others. What's the space? Who am I talking to? What are they
actually feeling about me? What do I think their pre-
conceptions are about me? What do they want to hear? What
kind of writer are they?

"Being on the other side of that handball court, how do
you make a harmonious collaboration? How well is it going
to accomplish what you're there for, which is to attract attention
to a piece of work that you've done?

"So, obviously, doing interviews is not a totally pleasant
thing. Every time I read one that I've done, it causes me a
certain amount of pain. But so do many other things I do as
an actor and a filmmaker."

Despite his reluctance to be interviewed, which he says · is balanced by his awareness that such interviews help attract a public for his work, Nicholson is serious and articulate once he is actually engaged in conversation about his work. He was clearly enthusiastic about "One Flew Over the Cuckoo's Nest," based on Ken Kesey's cult classic about free spirit Randall P. McMurphy's impact on the rigidly organized society of a metaphorical insane asylum. (The film went on to win Nicholson his first Oscar, as well as best film, best director for Milos Forman, and best actress for Louise Fletcher.) But to my surprise he also responded willingly and astutely to questions about his career and the film business in general.

"I've been very lucky as an actor over all," he grinned. "I sort of feel that it is not to an actor's best advantage to be successful early in his career, because no one's really that good at acting in films until he's done it for a while.

"I consider it lucky not to have been in a commercial success for most of my career — lucky in the sense that there was never much money involved in my films, and all of my instincts were in reaction to what my esthetic evaluation of the property was.

"I've sort of still got that same outlook. When I pick what I'm going to do next, the main consideration for me is where the challenge is. You know, what is there in this that I haven't done before? What is unpredictable? What is new about this character?

"That continues to be the challenge: How to go on, not so much not repeating yourself, because that shouldn't be taboo either, but how to continue to meet new challenges, to find some goal in them. Because if you're not growing as an actor, it's not much fun."

I have rarely interviewed a film actor with a better grasp of both the technical and aesthetic aspects of filmmaking. For example, I asked him at one point why the narrative viewpoint of the book — that of a pyschopathic Indian — had been changed in the film.

"I think one simple but central decision was made," he said. "The book is expressionistic. It is, as you say, written from the point of view of one of the characters, so it has a subjective point of view, from an Indian who is a schizophrenic. Therefore a lot of imagery is poetic in the way that schizophrenic imagery can be. I think Milos just decided to shoot the objective reality, which I think was the best way to approach this kind of material.

"I feel that the play was not really successful because it stopped all the time for long, long monologues of a non-dramatic nature, which is always difficult in the theatre, and 10 times more difficult in the cinema. Technically, the camera always functions best when it's just a cool, objective eye. That's recording reality, and what's going on inside the character's head is evoked by the images on the screen. And that's why I think the film works better than the play."

I had another aesthetic question for Nicholson before our interview ended — a question raised by the fact that the motion picture was actually filmed inside the Oregon State Hospital and that inmates worked in it as extras.

"When we see 'Cuckoo' on the stage," I suggested, "we are always aware that the inmates are actors pretending to be crazy. But while watching the film, I couldn't help wondering from time to time who among the characters were really insane and who were just acting insane."

Whereupon Nicholson fixed me with that Cheshire Cat grin, and drawled: "Well, I was confident which I was (pause), because I am well-known."

Happily, he still is.

Chapter 18

DIXIE CARTER & HAL HOLBROOK: THE TWAIN MEET

One celebrity this professional celebrity-seeker never had to seek was Dixie Carter. I knew her before she was a celebrity. In fact, E! The Entertainment Channel included me as one of the discoverers of this versatile multi-media star in its Celebrity Profile of her in 2000.

That was also the year my wife Tugar and I found ourselves sitting one evening with the elegantly gowned Dixie at her table in the ornate banquet hall of the Russian Embassy in Washington, D.C.

The event, presented on April 15, 2000, under the patronage of Ambassador Ushakov of the Russian Federation, and Mrs. Ushakov, was the annual William Shakespeare Award for Classical Theatre Gala, staged by Washington's world-class Shakespeare Theatre. Dixie, who had starred lustrously in the company's 1998 season opening production of Oscar Wilde's extremely difficult "A Woman of No Importance," was there to receive a Millenium Recognition Award from Artistic Director Michael Kahn. Other celebrities on hand for the big event included actors Elizabeth Ashley, Harry Hamlin, Kelly McGillis, and Tom Hulce, each also receiving a Millenium Award, and Sir Anthony Hopkins, winner of the annual "Will" Award for 2000.

Two years earlier, we had sat proudly with Dixie at a similar gala in Washington's historic Union Station when her husband, Hal Holbrook, received the 1998 "Will" Award, given in recognition of an entire career in classical theatre. Hal's acceptance speech was Shakespearean in its eloquence and majesty. Dixie's, two years later, was warm and gracious and dramatic and funny — all the things I had found her to be over the 40 years I have known her. As she spoke, I found myself remembering the very first time I had seen this now famous "designing woman" on the stage.

It was the summer of 1960 in Memphis, and the beautiful young college student from McLemoresville, TN, was making her professional debut at Front St. Theatre in the leading role of Julie Jordan in Rodgers & Hammerstein's musical masterpiece, "Carousel." Her leading man was Memphis actor/baritone George Hearn, who would go on to a brilliant Broadway career, winning Tonys and Emmys and, for about a year in the 1970s, winning Dixie herself as his bride. Dixie and George, as Julie and Billy, were so great in "Carousel" that I had trouble expressing my enthusiasm, and so resorted in my review to paraphrasing the show's wonderful love song, "If I Loved You."

Dixie Carter with George Hearn in her debut musical, "Carousel," in Memphis in 1960. (Author's collection)

"If I loved it (and HOW I loved it), words wouldn't come in an easy way…. How do I tell you," I wrote, "what heights of vocal artistry and what depths of feeling George Hearn and Dixie Carter pour into these roles?— Hearn, with his self-confident swagger, bolstered by the technique that only training and experience can provide. Miss Carter, groping now and then for the technique she does not yet have, yet somehow reaching the audience through instincts that always seem right and an inner glow which no amount of technique could replace or provide…."

Well, you get the idea. I thought this 19-year-old neophyte, Dixie Carter, was simply terrific — warm, beautiful, and a truly extraordinary talent. Over the next three years, I was never again at a loss for words to tell readers how much I loved her starring performances in a string of Front St. Theatre productions, including "Oklahoma!," "New Moon," "Babes in Arms," "Brigadoon," and "Mister Roberts." When Gladys Vaughan, borrowed from the late Joseph Papp's New York Shakespeare Festival, came to direct the Memphis Shakespeare Festival's 1963 spring production of "Much Ado About Nothing," and asked me (as festival co-founder and board member) to help her recruit a cast, I didn't hesitate. I urged her to try to get Dixie Carter and George Hearn.

She cast them both — Dixie as Hero and Hearn as Benedick. In my review, I said: "Miss Carter, known heretofore primarily as a singer, takes to Shakespeare like an Easter duck to water, and makes the gentlest and loveliest of Heros." Vaughan was so excited about both Memphis actors that she promised them roles in Papp's Shakespeare productions if they would move to New York.

Both did. Hearn was immediately cast in two Shakespeare-in-the-Park productions, but at first Dixie lacked the confidence to attempt Shakespeare in New York. Besides, she was really in New York to prepare for a career in grand opera. Her lifelong ambition had been to sing at the Metropolitan Opera, and she was crushed when it rejected her as not having a big enough voice. (A clumsy surgeon had damaged her vocal cords while performing a tonsillectomy on her when she was a child. Later doctors told her it was a wonder she could sing at all.)

I knew none of this at the time, but was proud when I heard on the theatrical grapevine that when Dixie finally gave in to Gladys Vaughan's entreaties and auditioned for Papp (who in 1988 would become the first winner of Washington's "Will" Award) he liked her so much that he cast her as Perdita in "A Winter's Tale," and commissioned David Amram to write a song especially for her to sing in the show. (Other emerging stars in that production included Michael Moriarty, James Earl Jones, Salome Jens, William Devane, Mitchell Ryan, Charles Durning and Roscoe Lee Browne.)

In 1967 I heard that, after a disappointing season understudying such stars as Patrice Munsel in Richard Rodgers' New York State Theatre company, Dixie had done a season of cabaret at Upstairs at the Downstairs, performing with two other promising unknowns, Lily Tomlin and the late Madeline Kahn. And then I heard that she had married a millionaire.

It was all true. She had married Wall Street investment banker Arthur Carter (later the founding publisher of The New York Observer), becoming Dixie Carter Carter, and gradually letting her career lapse. In 1969 daughter Ginna was born, and the next year, Mary Dixie.

I thought Dixie could have made it big, was disappointed when she gave up her career, and sort of forgot about her until one day in 1975. Tugar and I were getting out of a taxi at the corner of 50th St. and 8th Ave. in New York. Behind us I heard a familiar voice sing out, "Is that Edwin Howard getting out of that taxi?"

I looked back, and there was Dixie Carter, getting out of another taxi. I introduced her to Tugar and was sorry to hear she was divorced, but delighted to hear that her career was back on again. She was on her way to a rehearsal of "Jesse and the Bandit Queen," in which her portrayal of Belle Starr won her a Theatre World Award and restored some of the confidence she told us the marriage had cost her.

Joe Papp had come back into her life, too, with "Jesse and the Bandit Queen." For him she also appeared opposite Richard Chamberlain in "Fathers and Sons," and won a Drama Desk nomination. She was back in show business with both feet now, appearing in the TV soap opera, "The Edge of Night," during the day, and doing plays, such as Circle in the Square's revival of "Pal Joey," at night. Soon George Hearn had come back into her life, too, but their belated marriage was brief, marked by differences they just couldn't work out.

In 1979, Dixie worked for Papp again, in "Taken in Marriage," with a distinguished cast that included Colleen Dewhurst, Meryl Streep, Elizabeth Wilson, Nancy Marchand and Kathleen Quinlan. (She and Quinlan would work together again beginning in 1999 in the CBS dramatic series, "Family Law.")

Dixie was especially thrilled and moved to be appearing on the same stage with Dewhurst. "I had idolized her for years," she told me, "and here we were rehearsing together — she with shower thongs on her feet, and me with a lump in my throat."

In the audience on opening night were Paramount television producers Bob Bovette and Tom Miller, who picked Dixie out of that august company and offered her a contract and an ABC series called "Out of the Blue." Despite featuring Dixie and an angel, it was apparently ahead of its time and failed after four months. (Two decades later, "Touched by an Angel" was one of CBS's most popular shows.)

In the meantime, CBS kept looking for the right vehicle for Dixie, and came awfully close in 1982 with "Filthy Rich," a broad satire of "Dallas," "Dynasty," et al, set in good ole Memphis. Dixie and Delta Burke played hoop-skirted docents at the Mississippi River Museum on Mud Island. I loved it, and Dixie was terrific as the social-climbing Carlotta Beck, but the series only lasted one season. However, after the final episode ran, the series' writer, Linda Bloodworth-Thomason, erstwhile reporter and teacher from Poplar Bluff, Mo. (not far from Memphis), told Dixie that one day she was going to create a series for her that would be more mainstream.

Knowing that many promises are made in show business, and precious few are kept, Dixie went on about her career business. Back in New York, she was terrific in John Ford Noonan's play, "A Couple of White Chicks Sittin' Around Talkin'," which she did with Soap star/director Dorothy Lyman. (Supper with them after the performance was a hoot.) She played Gary Coleman's adoptive mother on

"Diff'rent Strokes" for a couple of years, and loved working with Conrad Bain. Then in 1983, Tugar and I saw her again onstage at Joe Papp's Public Theatre in Thomas Babe's newspaper comedy, "Buried Inside Extra." Her co-star was no less a luminary than Hal Holbrook, who had been crisscrossing the country for almost 30 years in his magnificent one-man show, "Mark Twain Tonight." In 1966 it had won him a Tony Award, a Drama Critics' Circle Award, and a 90-minute television special. And no doubt it contributed mightily to his being elected to Broadway's Theatre Hall of Fame in the year 2000.

I was not thrilled with "Buried Inside Extra," but thought the entire cast, including Sandy Dennis and Vincent Gardenia, performed with "such style and aplomb that the play's deficiencies were masked through much of the evening." As for Dixie and Hal, I wrote that when they were onstage, "it's like being at a particularly lively party," which is what our evening at the Public turned out to be.

I had scheduled a dressing-room interview with Dixie after the show, but when we got backstage she asked us to join her and Holbrook at the opening of cabaret singer Amanda McBroom's new nightclub act at Freddy's, an intimate little supper club on 49th St., east of Third.

In the course of a wonderful evening, I learned that Dixie had debuted her own cabaret act, with McBroom's arranger/accompanist Michelle Brourman also doing the honors for her, six months earlier at The Gardenia in Los Angeles, and that Dixie's act had already been booked for two weeks at Freddy's six months hence. Clearly, Dixie was reconnoitering a new career path.

First, though, she and Holbrook and "Buried Inside Extra" were opening in about a month and a half at London's prestigious Royal Court Theatre. Dixie's daughters, Ginna and Mary Dixie, were going to London with them, as was Holbrook's daughter Eve. And later Dixie's parents, Mr. and Mrs. Halbert Carter, would fly over and together they would all go to Austria where Dixie had arranged for her mother to take Ana Aslan's famed arthritis treatment at Ybbs, outside Vienna. (This was the first of repeated examples I would see over the next decade and a half of the lengths to which Dixie would go to insure the best available care and treatment for ailing family members.)

From all this family togetherness, we didn't have to be geniuses to figure out that Dixie and Hal, who had met while making the 1981 TV movie, "The Killing of Randy Webster," were planning to become co-stars in real life. At the time he met Dixie, Holbrook would later explain, "I was off women. I had had two failed marriages, and I was just off women.... I thought maybe we could just be friends. But she kept calling me Mr. Holbrook...."

The wedding took place in Dixie's hometown of McLemoresville, TN, with much fanfare and flowing champagne on Memorial Day, 1984. Tugar and I weren't able to be there for the ceremony, but a few months later in the beautiful back garden of their house in Bel Air, the four of us spent several hours ceremoniously consuming the last four bottles of their very good wedding champagne. I've never been very good at math, but I believe that came to somewhere around a bottle apiece, a record I am happy to say we have never broken in subsequent happy times in the Holbrooks' Los

Angeles homes and elsewhere.

I had first seen Holbrook perform in "Marco's Millions" and Arthur Miller's "After the Fall" with the new Lincoln Center Repertory Company in New York in 1963. Then in 1966, I saw him for the first time in his remarkable re-creation of Mark Twain on the lecture tours the brilliant humorist/satirist/philosopher undertook when he was 60 and continued off and on until his death at 75. In the course of a personal friendship with Holbrook over almost 20 years, my admiration for him has grown to awe. I am awed by him not only as an actor, but also as a dramatist, for in arranging Twain's varied writings into lecture programs, Holbrook is the dramatist as well as the performer. With an incredible 12 hours and more of Twain's written words committed to memory, he programs himself as each performance progresses, feeling each audience's responses as he goes, and sequencing the material accordingly.

Because Twain's writings are so eternally timely, Hal's selection of material sometimes involves deep soul-searching to make conscientious decisions. In 1991, right after the Gulf War began, I remembered that he had once included Twain's bitterly ironic "War Prayer" in one of his performances, and telephoned him to ask if he were going to use it again in the Gulf War context.

He was, he told me, but he had agonized over it: "I feel a heavy responsibility to support our troops and at the same time to stay true to what Twain would have said about the war. I opposed the Vietnam War, but I do not oppose the Gulf War, and my reason for doing the 'War Prayer' is simply to remind us, while supporting our troops, that war is not something to shout about, but a very sobering adventure."

In the written piece, Twain counterpointed a patriotic preacher's spoken prayer with its unspoken — and unspeakable — implications. But on the stage, Holbrook eliminated the dialectical argumentation and went straight to the heart of what Twain was saying — that when we pray for victory in war, we are asking God to do terrible things to other people.

Here is a slightly abbreviated version of Twain's "War Prayer" as it was so powerfully and devastatingly compressed onstage by Holbrook's Twain: "O Lord our Father, our young patriots, idols of our hearts, go forth to battle — be Thou near them!... O Lord our God, help us to tear THEIR soldiers to bloody shreds with our shells; help us to cover their smiling fields with the pale forms of their patriot dead... help us to drown the thunder of the guns with the shrieks of their wounded, writhing in pain; help us to lay waste their humble homes with a hurricane of fire;... help us to turn them out roofless with their little children to wander unfriended the wastes of their desolated land in rags and hunger and thirst,... for our sakes who adore Thee, Lord, blast their hopes, blight their lives, protract their bitter pilgrimage, make weary their steps... stain the white snow with the blood of their wounded feet! We ask it, in the spirit of love, of Him Who is the Source of Love...the ever-faithful refuge and friend of all that are sore beset and seek His aid with humble and contrite hearts. Amen."

Holbrook's Mark Twain has become much more than a theatrical impersonation. In times of crisis he IS Mark Twain, somehow resurrected to pace the lecture platforms of his beloved nation, reminding us with devastating wit and irony how far short of our religious, democratic and humanitarian ideals we still fall.

In appearance, Holbrook is uncannily like Twain, an effect achieved over the years with varying amounts of greasepaint, wigs and whiskers. After a performance in Memphis in the mid-1980s, I sat in his Malco Theatre dressing-room with him and watched him meticulously removing his make-up for what I remember as about an hour and a half. Ten years later at the Warner Theatre in Washington, I sat in his dressing-room with him after another of his Twain lectures, and it seemed to me he had his make-up off in no more than 20 or 30 minutes.

"The longer I do Twain," he observed wryly, "the less make-up I need." (CBS's 1967 Emmy-winning TV Special of Holbrook's "Mark Twain Tonight" was recently made available on video for the first time.)

I have also been amused and moved, and sometimes astonished, by the broad variety of Hal's performances on stage, screen and television. He is, as Washington's Shakespeare Theatre recognized in presenting him its "Will" Award, one of our finest classical actors. A few years ago, he did a highly praised King Lear at the Roundabout Theatre in New York. In 1999 in the Shakespeare Theatre's "Merchant of Venice," he created the most powerful, dignified and tragically believable Shylock I have ever seen. It brought the theatre the largest audience of any production in its history up to that time.

Unquestionably, Hal Holbrook and Dixie Carter have been good for each other — and for each other's careers.

Encouraged by Hal, Dixie's career as a cabaret singer

took off at Freddy's and led her to the top cabaret venue in the country, New York's Cafe Carlyle, where she was a reliable sign of spring over a 10-year period.

Two years after the Holbrooks married, Linda Bloodworth-Thomason made good on her promise and created for Dixie the funniest, most original and memorable TV sitcom character since Lucille Ball's Lucy Ricardo. The character was Julia Sugarbaker, and the show, "Designing Women," ran for seven seasons on CBS. In many parts of the country it is still being shown two or three times a day in syndication.

Dixie's Julia was smart, sassy, good-looking, opinionated, liberal, and sexy in a ladylike way. The show dealt with topical issues, and developed a superb ensemble cast — including Delta Burke as Julia's sister and partner in an interior decorating business which also employed Annie Potts, Jean Smart and a black ex-con played winningly by Meshach Taylor. There were also interesting guest stars including, intermittently, Hal Holbrook as Julia's boy friend, Reese, and Dixie's daughters, Ginna, also called Gigi, and Mary Dixie, by this time both Harvard graduates in theatre. Hal also made his directing debut on the series in 1988. When I interviewed Bloodworth-Thomason in 1989, she told me how much she admired Holbrook — "his comedy timing is the best I've ever seen," she said — and that she was creating a new half-hour series for CBS, probably to be called "Arkansas," especially for him. I've never found out exactly what happened, but when it premiered the next year it was still set in Arkansas, but called "Evening Shade" and starred Burt Reynolds as the local high school football coach with Holbrook in the supporting role of his father-in-law, publisher of the

Evening Shade Argus. Again Bloodworth Thomason and her producer/husband Harry Thomason assembled a fine ensemble cast, including Elizabeth Ashley, Ossie Davis, Charles Durning, Ann Wedgeworth, and another Memphis-trained actor, Michael Jeter. "Evening Shade" enjoyed a four-year run.

The Holbrooks were both at the top of their games all through the second half of the '80s and all of the '90s, and Tugar and I saw a lot of them in L.A., New York and Washington. We were in the audience for Dixie's first show at Cafe Carlyle when, after a cheering final ovation, she graciously thanked the management for letting her sing there, whereupon sister designing woman Annie Potts sang out, "Aw, forget it! They're lucky to have you!"

Indeed they were, and they knew it, and brought her back year after year to sing an astonishing range of playful, romantic, and sometimes heartbeaking songs by the Gershwins, Cole Porter, her friend and one-time voice coach John Wallowitch, Rodgers & Hart, Jerome Kern, Stephen Sondheim and even Bruce Springsteen and Bob Dylan.

We loved surprising her on the last night of her Carlyle engagement in 1998 by getting ourselves seated at a table that would be right under her nose when she stepped onto her little stage in front of the grand piano. She took us in with a momentarily surprised glance and, without missing a beat, worked us deftly into her act, declaring: "Tugar and Edwin Howard drank rather a lot of champagne last night, bless their hearts!..."

Did I mention that in the late '80s and early '90s Dixie also managed to produce a couple of best-selling "Unworkout" tapes demonstrating her yoga fitness routines, and to write (without the help of a ghost) a delightful memoir called "Trying to Get to Heaven: Opinions of a Tennessee Talker." Columnist Liz Smith called it "one of the most spiritually uplifting and life-affirming memoirs I have ever read, besides being vastly amusing and astonishingly candid. (What other actress would devote an entire chapter to her facelift?!)"

This is probably a good place to quote some other critics and columnists about Dixie's work, so you won't get the idea that I am too prejudiced to be a reliable judge of her performances. Here are a few other opinions:

*Variety's night club critic "Mars" on her 1990 opening at the Carlyle: "With more spice than a Cajun pepper, more romance than moonlight over the Mississippi, and more class than a Boston Brahmin, TV star Dixie Carter returns to this toney nitery....Seated atop the piano, her long legs pointed seductively toward the audience, Carter proceeds to practically make love to the 88s. It's highly erotic yet totally raucous."

*Stephen Holden, New York Times cabaret critic, on her 1998 Carlyle show: "Dixie Carter (is) the cabaret world's most elegantly funny cut-up.... a performer who inhabits a song totally while singing it, veering from madcap playfulness one minute to intense, teary-eyed romanticism the next."

*Tom Shales, Washington Post TV critic on the 1999 debut of CBS's "Family Law": "...Fortunately, a little later, Lynn gets help, a two-fisted attorney played fabulously by Dixie Carter, who looks like she'll have a high time with the role. (Her) credo: 'I hate men and I play very dirty.'"

*Ron Wertheimer, New York Times: "On the same night it presents Man as Lummox on 'Ladies Man,' CBS holds up Woman as Saint on 'Family Law.' And look: Dixie Carter is featured in both series. What's she going to do tomorrow, play second base for the Braves?"

And, while we're at it — before I tell you of Dixie's greatest triumph so far, and how Hal was instrumental in making it happen for her — note these New York critics' and columnists' appraisals of her 1997 Broadway portrayal of Maria Callas in "Master Class":

*Peter Marks, New York Times: ".... her creation is a worthy successor (to Zoe Caldwell). She makes a gutsy, funny Callas, a wounded survivor who turns to pedagogy to exorcise her demons.... Some of (her) best moments, oddly enough, are in what previously seemed the weakest points in the play.... It's a sympathetic portrayal yet less sentimental than that of her immediate predecessor, Patti Lupone, who made her demand for the audience's affection far too obvious.... 'Master Class' is not so much a play as an extended stand-up routine. As such, it requires a headliner with charisma and command. In Ms. Carter, it has one."

*Howard Kissel, New York Daily News: "Midway through the first act, Carter cradles her face in her hand. Her feline, seductive eyes make her look uncannily like Callas.... What is most impressive about her characterization is the reservoir of emotion she draws on in the two great monologues McNally has written toward the close of each act, in which Callas shares her most searing memories.... Carter emerges from both monologues with tears streaming down her cheeks, and she makes the speeches themselves extremely moving....(She) has brought great intelligence and strength to the role. She has captured McNally's Callas sharply...."

Here's how Dixie Carter got the role that remains, at

this writing in 2001, the high point of her extraordinary career:

In 1993, she returned to Memphis to play Blanche DuBois, a role with which she had long identified, in a production of Tennessee Williams' "A Streetcar Named Desire," directed by her Front St. Theatre mentor, George Touliatos. Husband Hal Holbrook, though his own work schedule prevented his seeing an actual performance of "Streetcar," flew in and watched three hours of rehearsals. He was so impressed that he called his friend, producer Robert Whitehead, in New York and said, "You must go to Memphis and see my wife in 'Streetcar.'"

"Whitehead never made it to Memphis," Dixie told me later, "but three years later he remembered that phone call from Hal Holbrook, and he trusted that."

By late 1996, Whitehead needed another star to take over the role of Maria Callas in "Master Class." Hal had seen Whitehead's wife, Zoe Caldwell, in the play, and had tried to get Dixie to go back with him and see it. "I'm telling you," he said, "I see you in every word, every gesture. I see you on that stage. This part was written for you, Dixie, and somewhere, sometime, you will do this part."

By the time Hal got her to New York to see it, Caldwell had left "Master Class" and Lupone was playing it. Dixie told me she left the theatre knowing she had "seen something quite wonderful," but then forgot about it until the phone rang in her L.A. home just before Christmas ('96). It was Whitehead's office in New York, asking her if she would take over the Callas role in "Master Class" at the end of January.

The actress who had dreamed of a career at the Met and had idolized Maria Callas was going to play her on the Broadway stage!

Here is some of what I wrote about her performance in "Master Class," which opens with Callas telling a young opera hopeful that there is no being at center stage as if by magic:

"The 'magic' that has put Dixie Carter at center stage here at the Golden Theatre with her name above the title on the marquee, and her magnificent performance on the lips of thousands who have seen it since she took over the starring role two months ago, is more than 35 years of the kind of dedication and hard work which she, as Callas, pinpoints as 'discipline, technique and "Mut"' (the German word for courage)...

"I know the courage it took to take on this role — one of the most demanding in contemporary theatre, and one for which one of America's most celebrated actresses, Zoe Caldwell, had already won the Tony as the 1995-96 season's best actress.

"I know the vocal technique she had to develop to be able to speak almost continuously for two hours, projecting to the back of the balcony, without amplification. I know the discipline it takes day after day and night after night to sustain her energy and protect her newly deepened and strengthened voice through eight performances a week.

"I also came to the theatre knowing that the depth of Dixie's talents was probably still unplumbed. After she had shone so brightly in Rodgers & Hammerstein musicals and Shakespeare comedies in the 1960s, hadn't she won awards in dramatic roles at Joseph Papp's Public Theatre? Hadn't she surprised us with the extraordinary comedic gifts that made 'Designing Women' a long-running hit on television? And then

The Howards join the Holbrooks in the lobby of the Shakespeare Theatre in Washington after their benefit performance in "Love Letters" in 1999. Holbrook is still wearing his "Merchant of Venice" beard. (Photo courtesy of Anna Ng Delort)

hadn't she wowed us with her cabaret act?...

"So I knew Dixie would be good....but I was still bowled over by the extraordinary strength, subtlety, elegance and grandeur of her portrayal....

"There were times during McNally's marvelous play when I got the eerie feeling that Callas herself had somehow taken possession of Carter's body and was passionately re-living these crucial episodes in her life.... In each of the long soliloquies that climax the play's two acts, the actress herself is moved to tears in the process of moving us...(and) she speaks the lines of Lady Macbeth's aria in the 'Letter Scene' so compellingly that you are convinced she has sung them....

"Carter is also electrifying in her sheer-physical presence

The Holbrooks in a sentimental moment after a performance of "Merchant of Venice" at Washington's Shakespeare Theatre. (Author's collection)

on the stage. Dressed in an expensive black pantsuit with a large silk scarf elegantly draped around her shoulders, she moves with the purposeful precision of a ballerina, and uses her hands as eloquently as she does the organ tones of her voice...."

A year later, as we talked about her "Master Class" run, Dixie said: "Edwin, I don't know if you can imagine what that was like for me. I missed out on the Met, but it was almost like I got to sing on the stage at La Scala. It was the high point of my professional life, the only great role.... I'm sorry to burst into tears, but I know you understand. I couldn't believe they would entrust a role like that to a sitcom actress like me."

I tried to console her. "You're going to get more great roles," I said.

About four months later, The Washington Post carried

the news: Michael Kahn, artistic director of Washington's Shakespeare Theatre, had selected Dixie Carter to play the challenging title role in Oscar Wilde's "A Woman of No Importance," opening Sept. 1.

And now, a year and a half later, here we were in the Russian Embassy listening to Dixie Carter's gracious, witty and charming acceptance of the Shakespeare Theatre's Millenium Recognition Award. She had not only become a great cabaret and TV sitcom star; she had become a woman of some importance in the American theatre. And she was married to TWO of the theatre and film's finest performers: Hal Holbrook and Mark Twain.

Chapter 19

ARTHUR RUBINSTEIN: SPINE-TINGLING INFORMATION

When you're listening to a great singer, violinist or pianist, and suddenly get gooseflesh — those little shuddering chills up and down your spine (without which, the late Fritz Kreisler said, no musical performance is worthwhile) — you can be sure that the artist is getting it too.

My authority for this claim is none other than the great concert pianist, Arthur Rubinstein, who had already given gooseflesh to millions all over the world when I interviewed him in Memphis in 1971. He was 84 at the time, had been playing professionally for 73 years, and had another five years to go on his career before, nearly blind, he voluntarily ended it with a concert in Carnegie Hall in March of 1976.

Rubinstein had first performed in Memphis in 1939 and once each decade thereafter, but his final appearance there in

Arthur Rubinstein, at age 84, warming up in a drafty backstage area before his 1971 Memphis concert. (Photo courtesy of the University of Memphis Libraries' special collection)

1971 was the only time I got to sit down and ask him questions about his career and the nature of musical artistry in general.

Of those tingles up and down the spine, he assured me:

"If you feel it, you can be sure that the performer is feeling it twice as much. Only the other day in a concert I was playing a Schubert sonata and tears came to my eyes and I was so deeply moved I almost lost control. That is what you feel in the audience — the emotion which the performer feels from the work and transmits through it."

Then I asked Rubinstein his opinion of the relative importance of the composer and the interpreter, or performer, of a piece of music: "How much of the beauty is in the composer's symbols on paper, and how much in the hands and heart of the performer?"

"That is a question which interests me very much," he said. "In fact I have written a whole chapter about it in my memoirs. But I hope you will forgive me if I do not answer it here, because it is a very complicated question and I could not do it justice in a few words. Also, I want to keep something back for my book so you will read it."

For the same reason, the 84-year-old pianist also begged off telling about "the several beautiful women who almost wrecked my career" when he was a young man, promising that the book would tell all.

"But only to the age of 30," he added slyly. "I have already written 750 closely lined pages in long hand, and I am not out of my 20s yet. I expect to have the book finished in another two or three months, and ready to turn over to my publisher, Alfred Knopf. That is one of the nice things about living so long. You can tell about your youth because there is no one left to be hurt by it. But I do not think it would be nice to take my life much beyond 30, you know."

He ended up writing two books, about which more in

a minute. In both, he discussed the subject of the relative importance of the composer and interpreter of a piece of music. In brief, he said that performing music is "a personal dialogue with the composers." Expanding on the theme, he said: "We interpreters have something in common with painters. If you have a portrait done by 10 different painters, you will look different in each one. . . . Each of us brings to a work of music his own talents and tools, making the best of it through his own understanding, and developing his interpretation of it according to his own unique personality."

It was not until he married at the age of 43, Rubinstein confided to me at the age of 84, that he became a really good pianist, critics and audiences to the contrary notwithstanding.

"Oh, I was always a good musician," he said. "I always loved music, but playing the piano was only a means to enjoying music. I always hated to practice. But when I married, I got down to work. I didn't want my family to be disappointed in me."

The astonishingly vigorous and vital octogenarian was still playing a hundred concerts a year all over the world in the 1970s. "If I stay in one place more than two weeks," he said, "I get restless."

How, I wondered, did a man of his age maintain the physical wellbeing and mental discipline necessary for the rigorous schedule he set himself?

"Discipline?" he scoffed. "I know nothing of discipline. To me, the man who gets up every morning and goes to work at a bank, and counts out so much money in this pile and so much in that pile, has much more mental discipline than I do. That is something I could never keep straight. I hate money, anyway. I don't ever like to think about it. I only like the things it will buy."

Surprisingly for a man still practicing his profession at the age of 84, Rubinstein told me he approved forcible retirement at age 65 in business and industry. "It must be done, "he said, "to make way for the young. There are so many of them. If we don't get out of their way, I am afraid one day they will line us all up and — Bang! — shoot us."

But that facetiously posed prospect clearly was not worrying this delightful artist and raconteur. He was still getting a bang out of life and giving little or no thought to death or retirement. Amazingly, by age 84 he said he had played concerts in every country in the world except one: Tibet. It was an omission he explained with a continental shrug: "There are no pianos in Tibet."

Although proud of his honors and decorations from many countries, Rubinstein didn't like to dwell on past accomplishments — or failures.

"Every day is new," he told me. "You have to live it, and not even think about the past. What you did yesterday is nothing. What you do today is everything."

☆ ☆ ☆

True to his word, Rubinstein published a volume of hand-written memoirs two years after our interview. "My Young Years" (Knopf, 1973, 478 pages, with illustrations) was on the best-seller lists for three months. As he had said, it took him only up to age 30. But the book's success inspired Knopf to persuade him to write another book about the rest of his life, entitled "My Many Years." Because of his diminished eyesight, he had to dictate this one. It took him two years to complete and ran, with photos, to 626 pages. When he finished it, he wrote, "It made me love life more than ever, at the ripe age of 92." In 1982, at the age of 95, he died.

Reading Rubinstein can be wonderfully entertaining and informative, but the essential Rubinstein lies not between the covers of his two books but in the grooves of the astonishing number of piano recordings he left us. Not long after his death, BMG Classics released "The Rubinstein Collection," his entire recorded legacy, comprised of 94 compact discs containing 706 recordings of 347 different compositions. The re-mastered collection begins with his first 78s, recorded in the 1920s, and ends with his final recorded performances circa 1976. The last time I checked, the collection was priced at about $1,300.

Chapter 20

THE DANCING YEARS: ASTAIRE, KELLY, POWELL

At lunch one day in 1975 on Stage 20 of Metro-Goldwyn-Mayer's Culver City Studios, retired dance star Eleanor Powell disillusioned me about the apparent spontaneity of tap-dancing in movie musicals.

Miss Powell and the machine-gun tapping of her talented toes illuminated "Broadway Melody" (1936), "Rosalie" ('37), "Born to Dance" ('42), "Thousands Cheer" ('43), and many other film musicals between the mid-1930s and mid-'50s.

The same day I was lucky enough to draw her as my luncheon partner at a press party for the launching of MGM's musical compendium, "That's Entertainment II," Fred Astaire said of her, "She was a big star when I came over to Metro to do that first picture with her, and I knew I was going to have to hoof like mad because she dances like mad!" And Gene Kelly declared: "I run her films all the time, because if there is a reincarnation I feel that I would like to steal some of her steps!"

At the time I lunched with her, Powell was 65 and long-retired, but she still bubbled effervescently and seemed to radiate light from her shining eyes and sparkling teeth as she talked about the old days at MGM and the dance numbers that had been revived in 1974's "That's Entertainment" and its upcoming sequel.

I had been covering movies for almost 30 years when I sat down to lunch with Miss Powell, and I thought I knew everything there was to know about how movies were made. In musicals, I knew of course that in front of the cameras, the actors mouthed the lyrics of their songs to playbacks of recordings they had made earlier in sound studios. But I never knew that the exuberant, spontaneous-sounding tap-tap-tapping of Eleanor and Fred and Gene's dancing feet was dubbed in after all the scenes had been filmed.

How in the world, I asked her, could a dancer exactly duplicate, months later, the tap sounds danced on-camera?

"Well," she grinned, "we watched ourselves on a screen as we dubbed them in — and we were good at it. You see, everything was done four times. First we'd go to the rehearsal hall and make up the number. You were your own choreographer. No. 2, you'd go into this big room where the orchestra was, and you'd make a take of just the music. You'd have to keep going over the routine with the orchestra wearing your little ballet slippers — for silence — because there'd be tempo changes, and the conductor wouldn't know them till you showed him. So you'd go over and over it. We used to be in that room with the orchestra up to 16 hours at a whack.

"No. 3, you'd go down on the set where, when you're not rehearsing or recording, you're doing the drama part of the movie, and you'd shoot the number to the playback of the recorded music. But you'd shoot it silent. And when you were shooting, there were bleachers on the set, and Mr. (Louis B.) Mayer (studio head) and all his relatives, and your friends and your son or daughter, and this whole crowd would come and sit and talk and laugh and smoke and cough or whatever. And you're out there in front of them, doing your number. But it's great because you've got an audience, and that hypes you up. I always loved an audience.

"And then, No. 4, you would go in after the picture was through shooting, and put the taps in. And, just like Bing Crosby singing, we would need only one or two takes in dubbing a number. Fred and I would need at most two takes to dub in the taps. It would usually be three months between the time you shot it and the time you dubbed in the taps, and you had to keep it all in mind.

"You're all alone, except for two technicians with earphones, watching yourself dance on a big screen, and they're playing the music very low to give you something to follow, and you do it — you reproduce on a platform precisely the same taps you did before so they can record them and dub them into the movie.

"So you see," she concluded with a laugh, "you can't call tap-dancers dumb!"

I said I never had and never would.

Just before our lunch together, I had watched Miss Powell, Astaire, Kelly, Ginger Rogers, Cyd Charisse, Leslie Caron, and other dancers in sequences from "That's

Entertainment II," and noticed that most tap-dancers — and especially Miss Powell — seemed almost always to smile as they danced.

Was that a standing order, I wondered, to smile — no matter how strenuous the routine?

Miss Powell's big smile spread even more broadly across her face as she replied:

"Honey, nobody ever told anybody to smile. If you see someone smiling while dancing, it's because they were just having a ball up there — havin' the time of their life. They might do it a thousand times, but they were still havin' fun.

"Maybe we should bring tap-dancing back. Maybe we could substitute dancin' for dope, 'cause you can get just as high on dancin', honey, as anybody could ever want to go. You don't need nothin' else!"

After lunch with Eleanor Powell that day over a quarter-century ago, I learned some more about dancing in movie musicals from Astaire, then 75, and Kelly, a youngster of 63. By 1975, both had retired from dancing, though both were still active in movies from time to time — Astaire in straight acting roles, and Kelly as actor and director.

Doing the time step, as it were, with these two great screen stars was one of my more memorable experiences in half a century on the movie beat. Separately, I asked each the same series of questions. Here are highlights from my questions and their answers:

Why don't you dance anymore?

KELLY (who suffered a knee injury while skiing in 1958): "I just don't. No, I don't even dance to work out. I play tennis."

ASTAIRE: "Dance? For what? What am I gonna do it for? I know a lot of professional golfers who don't play golf anymore. I understand why they don't. It's...Well, it just becomes a job."

Do you have any particular favorites among your films, or favorite numbers in them?

KELLY: "I like very much 'On the Town' because we sort of changed the style of doing musicals with that. But it's not a public all-time favorite. It's a little dated now, I guess, because it's been imitated. But it meant a lot to me at the time."

ASTAIRE: "I have had some trick numbers which I liked very much. I liked one particularly that was very complicated to do — the one in 'Royal Wedding' in which I danced on the walls and ceiling. And I always liked the 'Top Hat' number. I don't see many of my old films, because I don't look for them. But once in a while there is something on and I see it and say, 'That's not bad, you know.'"

Have you ever committed yourself to naming your favorite dance partner? Or would that be too much like committing suicide?

KELLY: "Sure. I don't mind. My favorite partner has always been Fred Astaire."

ASTAIRE: "We actually only did one number together — 'The Babbitt and the Bromide' ('Ziegfeld Follies,' 1946) — but Gene is always kind enough to say that. It gets him off the hook. Of course, he could say the Mouse from the 'Tom & Jerry' cartoons, which he danced with in 'Anchors Aweigh.'

"Of course, working with all those lovely gals, neither of us can suddenly say, 'Well, So-and-So's better,' or 'I liked

Eleanor or Ginger (Rogers) or Cyd (Charisse) or Rita (Hayworth) best. So I never have. Or I say Bing Crosby. You know, we danced together in 'Holiday Inn.' I've got a string that long — all these great gals, and I would hate to leave anybody out. They were all wonderful dancers, but all different. It's just not possible to say who was best."

Question to Astaire only: How did you work out your solo and partnered numbers?

ASTAIRE: "You get ideas just by experimenting, thinking things out. Sometimes they come to you while you're walking along the street. It's like anybody writing anything. I write songs sometimes, and I get a melody when I least expect it. If you get stuck for a dance number, you go into a rehearsal hall and just mess around until you get something that works. You say, wait a minute, I need a chair — two chairs. And you work it out. You say, what about a ladder? And you just use props that occur to you or fit into the situation. We used a cow in 'Funny Face' because one setting was a little country road and a cow could easily have walked through. So I did a bullfighting dance. It wasn't a bad number. I liked it. That's the way things happen. A cane is a good prop. You slap it down, make a noise with it, catch it, throw it up, let it hit the ground. I used to love to do that."

And when you worked with a partner?

ASTAIRE: "If there are two people in a number, you have somebody subbing for the female star as you work it out. We used to call those girls 'work horses.' The star lady was always at a fitting or the hair-dresser's, so we would work out the routine with the 'work horse,' and she would explain or demonstrate the steps to the star later."

Did the 'work horse'...?

ASTAIRE (interrupting): "That's not a very nice expression."

But I got it from you!

ASTAIRE: "Yes I know, but I'm kinda sorry I said it. I meant that we used to say, all right, we're going to put this together, and we'd work with what we might better call the understudy. Ginger wasn't always available at the time we needed to work out the numbers. But when it came down to actually learning it, she approved this, or didn't like that, or felt she couldn't do the other thing. Then we'd try to make everybody happy, and do it."

You choreographed all your own numbers, didn't you?

ASTAIRE: "On a couple of occasions I had help. If I would get stuck, I would call in Bob Alton or Hermes Pan and say, 'Here, what can we do here?' Or 'Gee, I don't know how to get this number started. What do you think?' And they would get me started. It's not possible for a choreographer to take a whole routine and put it on for me, because I couldn't work that way. Most dancers, I think, are the same way. I think Gene does the same thing. You like help when you need it. Bob Alton used to come up with some very good ideas. But the final effort is something you put together yourself. So...that's the hoofer's story."

Do movie musicals have a future?

ASTAIRE: "I don't know. The music is different now, of course. You can dance to rock and roll; I could dance to anything if I liked it. But it's a different kind of thing. I don't know."

KELLY: "I think it's very difficult today to make musical films because they need music that's conducive to real dancing, and we're still dealing with rock. Everybody says it's passing, but it has not passed, as you can see by record sales. But you see better dancing in the discotheques than you do in films, because it's improvisation and everybody's a star in a discotheque. Your date's over in the corner and you're over here, and you wave at each other, and you're both stars. Economics isn't the only reason they don't make musicals. The music is one of the main reasons they don't make musicals anymore."

Kelly was right. MGM's musical and dance compendiums — its three "That's Entertainments" and its 1985 "That's Dancing" — are treasured, wonderfully nostalgic, and loving obituaries for the movie musical, surely the liveliest of the lively arts. Ironically, Kelly himself had helped bury it with the 1980 film, "Xanadu" (which I think of as the last movie musical) in which he co-starred with Olivia Newton-John, Sandahl Bergman, and a young Memphis actor named Michael Beck.

Fred Astaire died of pneumonia in 1987 at the age of 88, Kelly died of a stroke in 1996 at the age of 84, and Powell died in 1982 at the age of 72. But thanks to television's movie channels — our living museum of the cinematic arts — we can still enjoy the lost art of the movie musical.

And we can still see the three of them from time to time, still tap-tap-tapping, and nearly always smiling — because, as Miss Powell assured me 25 years ago, "they were havin' the time of their life."

Chapter 21

LILLIAN GISH: THE 'LAST' INTERVIEW

When I was able to lure Lillian Gish into a quiet corner to spend 45 minutes with me and my tape recorder in Chicago in 1978, I was of course thrilled to meet this lovely link with the pioneer past of motion pictures — "the first lady of the silent screen." I was also completely charmed by the 82-year-old actress. When my subsequent two-part interview appeared in my Front Row column in The Memphis Press-Scimitar, I confess to having nurtured a rather smug hunch that mine was probably going to be the last major interview done with this great star of stage and screen. She had come out of a long retirement to appear in Robert Altman's "The Wedding," and I suspected that Chicago's benefit premiere of the film might be her last press appearance.

Six years later, The Press-Scimitar died, and for a while

there I didn't feel so good myself. But Lillian Gish seemed eternal. In 1986-7 — at the age of 90 and 91 — she appeared in two more movies, playing Alan Alda's addled mother in "Sweet Liberty," and poignantly co-starring with Bette Davis in Lindsay Anderson's "The Whales of August."

When I met Miss Gish at the "Wedding" benefit premiere in Chicago that summer of 1978, I was enchanted, and amazed to discover that the serene loveliness and benign authority that suffused the screen more than half a century earlier in D. W. Griffith's "Broken Blossoms," "Way Down East," and "Orphans of the Storm" were as palpable as ever. Even the innate aura of purity — substantiated by her enduring spinsterhood — remained.

The late Alexander Woollcott wrote of the actress as Camille: "There was around Miss Gish a strange mystic light that was not made by any electrician." As she and I sat together on little gold chairs in Chicago's Drake Hotel ballroom, that mystic light still seemed to shine in her eyes.

Our conversation began on the mundane level of why she had chosen to come out of retirement to appear live on the screen for no more than two minutes and spend the rest of the film as a corpse.

"Well," she smiled benignly, "I've always picked people for talent, and Mr. Altman came up to my house and told me the story of his film and said, 'You die, but it's going to be amusing.' Well, that was intriguing! I have died a lot of times, but it never was amusing. So that aroused my curiosity.

"It reminded me a little of when Guthrie McClintic told me how he wanted me to play Ophelia opposite John Gielgud's Hamlet on Broadway years ago (1936). Ophelia died, too, of course, and it wasn't funny, but I thought I would play her as just another innocent child of the sort I played on the screen. But Guthrie said, no, I was going to be a lewd Ophelia.

"Well, that was intriguing, too! So we did make her a lewd Ophelia, and got wonderful reviews. Everybody understood it, and doctors used to come back and say, 'How did you know that a mind like this would go the opposite direction when it became diseased? They all said it was true.

"So I was intrigued by what Mr. Altman said about my death being amusing. I didn't know him well enough to know how he had discovered that he could make death funny. But I knew that things are not always what they seem. I know that my sister Dorothy and I used to always weep at weddings. They seemed sad to us because you never knew how it would turn out."

Dorothy, who appeared with Lillian in many of their early silent films, died in 1969, and Lillian, who lived to be 99, never married. Billed as Baby Lillian, the elder Gish sister made her debut at the age of 5 in Risingsun, Ohio, in a road company of "In Convict's Stripes." When Lillian was 16, she and year-younger Dorothy visited their friend, Gladys Smith, who had begun calling herself Mary Pickford, at the old Biograph Studio in New York. Pickford introduced them to Griffith, the Kentucky-born director who virtually invented the motion picture as an art form, and together they made movie history.

In the few weeks before I interviewed her, Gish's schedule would have exhausted an ordinary person. She had flown to Tahiti, boarded the QE2, and lectured aboard it while cruising via Australia to Los Angeles; taped her own TV special there called "Infinity In an Hour;" flown to New York to introduce her 1926 silent film of "La Boheme" to the Metropolitan Opera Guild at Town Hall; flown back to California to finish her special, appear on the final Carol Burnett Show and tape a salute to Henry Fonda; appeared with a symphony orchestra to introduce its performance of the background music for a showing of her 1919 film, "Broken Blossoms," and then flown to Chicago for the "Wedding" benefit.

How, I wondered, could she maintain such a schedule and still look so calm and serene?

"I'm a workaholic," she said. "Beginning at the age of 5, I got into the bad habit of just working. I have had no life of my own. Every now and again I think of it and resent it. But you just give over. Everything's a habit, I suppose. And in films when I started, we worked 12 hours a day, seven days a week. In my work, we had no social life. We never met anyone outside our studio because we didn't go to lunch or dinner out where you might meet people.

"You see, I came out of a school where you were expected to be a craftsman. You had to know all about everything. You rehearsed for weeks and weeks. 'Birth of a Nation' — months. 'Way Down East' — eight solid weeks of rehearsal, from 10 in the morning till 6 at night, over and over until you knew it backwards. You only rehearsed a stage play three weeks."

But there was no dialogue in silent movies — no lines to learn or rehearse, were there?

"There were no scripts of any kind with Griffith. But you had to know to the split second how much time you had for each scene and where the camera was going to be. If it was going to be here, one kind of acting; back there, you acted with your whole body.

Each role, the actress told me, presented a different challenge: "If you didn't have the imagination, you couldn't do it. When I had to die of TB as Mimi in 'La Boheme,' I went to the priest at the county hospital and he took me through the wards where the patients would cough for me. I had never seen anyone die. You have to watch the human race. You can't just look into your own life and think, 'How did I feel when such and such happened?' You can't move an audience with that. You can't move them with your own tears, either. It's up to you to make THEM cry, not YOU cry.

"You have to have the imagination and resourcefulness to investigate life. During the making of 'Birth of a Nation,' Griffith would tell us, 'It isn't enough for you to know what was going on in America. You must read history and know what was going on in the rest of the world.'

"Be a people watcher. Never stop. And you'll learn to act that way."

I asked Miss Gish if she had a favorite role or performance over her long career. She thought for a moment, then replied firmly, "I never played a part where I could realize everything I had in mind for the character. I don't think of myself as a person. I think of myself as a painter. I have a piece of canvas. I don't have oil or water colors. I only have this (she touches her face) and this (her body), and I paint a character with them. But I never get it right, so I haven't got a favorite."

How, I wondered, did the actress stay such a picture of health?

"I've lived in New York off and on since I was 5," she said, "and I've lived abroad. Over here, we're interested in sickness; over there, they're interested in health. They know the importance of change. If they live in the mountains, they go to the sea for their health. If they live on the sea, they go to the mountains.

"Since I live in New York at sea level, I go to the mountains. I go to the Alps — the Austrian Alps, because the Austrians are a peaceful people. It's the only place in the world that you can be walking in the woods and a strange person walks by and smiles and says to you, 'Bless God!' No one's rich. No one's poor. They're all about even. So that's where I go in the summertime."

There was not a line of regret in Miss Gish's lovely face, so I did not ask what she might have regretted in her long, single life of work and fame. But I couldn't resist asking, if she had had a child, what one present she would have wanted to give that son or daughter.

"Oh," she smiled without hesitation, "I'd have to say curiosity. That makes for a happy life. Then you're never bored. Time is your friend. Boredom is your enemy. If you keep interested, you keep alive."

Lillian Gish kept alive until Feb. 27, 1993, when, at the age of 97, she passed away quietly in her sleep. I am sure she died a good death; she had had so much practice — as Ophelia in "Hamlet," Mimi in "La Boheme," and so many other roles.

Lillian Gish never married, though she was determinedly courted for some years by the New York theatre critic, George Jean Nathan. I thought, too, from the way she wrote about him in her 1969 autobiography, "The Movies, Mr.

Griffith, and Me," that she had a great affection for her mentor, D.W. Griffith.

Her last words to me on that evening in 1978 when we sat and talked after the premiere of "The Wedding," expressed her own deep confirmation of what Griffith had told her about the acting profession.

"He said," she confided, "'What you get is a living. What you give is a life.'"

Lillian Gish is interviewed by the author at an afternoon press conference in Chicago during the 1978 premiere of Robert Altman's "The Wedding."
(Author's collection)

Chapter 22

THE DIRECTORS

It is the stars who lure us to the movies, but it is the directors who make the movies, and often make the stars.

In my half-century of seeing stars, I have also seen some of the industry's greatest directors up close and at work.

Clarence Brown, who directed Garbo in her greatest films, worked very subtly and quietly behind the camera while directing William Faulkner's "Intruder in the Dust" on locations around Oxford, Miss., in 1949. At the premiere, Faulkner said what he liked most about the film was its quiet moments — "so quiet you could hear the crickets chirping." It was Faulknerian chirping, of course.

Cecil B. DeMille filmed the scene I watched being shot for "The Greatest Show on Earth" rather in the manner of a circus ringmaster, using expansive gestures and speaking from

Clarence Brown is greeted by the author at Memphis Airport as the famed director travels to Oxford, Miss. to direct the 1949 film version of William Faulkner's "Intruder in the Dust." (Author's collection)

time to time through a megaphone (in 1951).

John Ford and Henry Hathaway both operated like field generals, striding around location sites, barking orders. Ford, whom I watched at work on "The Horse Soldiers" in 1958, had no time for visiting press. A snarled "Hello!" and a distracted handshake were all I got from him in two days on location at Natchitoches, La. No matter. In such films as "Stagecoach," "The Fugitive," "The Grapes of Wrath," "The Informer" and "The Young Mr. Lincoln," he taught generations of moviegoers how to see. He also tried to teach his protege, John Wayne, how to direct, in the course of making "Horse Soldiers." I watched him sit by and let Wayne supervise routine scenes, but when a big scene like the blowing up of a wooden bridge with mounted cavalrymen riding across it came up, Ford took over and ran things like the lieutenant commander he was in World War II. The next year, Wayne did try his hand at directing, but his "The Alamo" suggested that he hadn't fully absorbed Ford's lessons, and "Green Berets" left no doubt.

When I visited the location site of "Nevada Smith," starring Steve McQueen, in the bayou country around Port Vincent, La., I didn't even get from Henry Hathaway the growled "Hello!" and distracted handshake I got from Ford. Hathaway had a way with him all right. He was clearly more interested in exposing film than exposing himself and his company to the prying eyes of a newsman.

When publicist Jim Merrick introduced me to him, he peered skeptically out from under a crumpled cloth hat and growled: "Memphis? How much circulation you got?" When I told him 150,000, Merrick added nervously, "And they're all movie fans." Hathaway had already moved on.

There was no question, though, about Hathaway's command of the medium. I saw him shoot five different camera set-ups in less than three hours, tyrannizing extras and bit players like a top sergeant. That's more than many directors shoot in a day. And I remain a great admirer of such Hathaway films as "Lives of a Bengal Lancer" (one of my favorite films as a child), "The Desert Fox," "Call Northside 777" and "True Grit."

Another great motion picture logistics expert was Sir Carol Reed, whose "Fallen Idol," "Odd Man Out," and "The Third Man" belong on any creditable list of the best films of all time. The film I watched him at work on — "The Agony and the Ecstasy" — was certainly not one of his best, but the scene

Huge blocks of marble dot the floor of Italy's La Mossa Quarry, as British director Sir Carol Reed stages a key sequence in 1965's "The Agony and the Ecstasy." (Author's collection)

I got to watch him stage in 1964 was filmed on one of the most exotic and historic of all movie locations.

It was the La Mossa Quarry high in the marble mountains above Carrara, Italy — the quarry to which Michelangelo himself journeyed to select the block of marble from which he would carve his great Moses. The quarry scene dramatized that very event, with Charlton Heston as the great sculptor. In real life it took Michelangelo eight months to find the right marble. For the film, Sir Carol and his crew (with Producer Darryl F. Zanuck himself on-site, having flown over from Hollywood, perhaps to keep an eye on the budget) blasted the great chunk of marble out of the quarry wall in a single, memorable afternoon.

I caught a brief glimpse of another great English director in action in 1966 on a rainy night in Dorset. The film was Thomas Hardy's "Far from the Madding Crowd," and the director was John Schlesinger. While I was chatting with Julie Christie in her dressing-room inside Bathsheba Everdene's Jacobean manor house, Schlesinger stuck his head in just long enough to shout: "Make it to Medical Aid to Vietnam!," then disappeared.

She jumped up and ran toward the door, calling, "John! What is it? Say it again!" He re-appeared and repeated, "Make it Medical Aid to Vietnam!"

Julie came back to her make-up table, sat down, pulled out a checkbook and starting writing — presumably a check for Medical Aid to Vietnam. "I always give five pounds," she confided, "no matter what it is. Five pounds doesn't sound like much in itself, but when you send five pounds in answer to 30 or 40 requests a year, it mounts up."

I didn't see Schlesinger again, but when the vastly underrated film came out the next year I could see why he was so busy that night. The scene was simply of Christie as Bathsheba looking out the window and seeing her faithful shepherd, Gabriel Oak, played by Alan Bates, struggling to tie down the rick-cloths and save her hay-ricks from the downpour. We arrived at the location at 8:30 p.m. The grips, prop men, cameramen and gaffers had been working since 5 p.m. to set up the scene. The actors had come from their hotels in Weymouth at 7, but the scene still wasn't ready two and a half hours later — delayed by a semi-trailer truck pulling a wind machine that couldn't be coaxed through the black gumbo mud coating the hillside.

We left after an hour, and Schlesinger still hadn't gotten the scene underway. But when the film came out, there it was, all breathtakingly real. Bates's Gabriel Oak was magnificent with the wind and the rain in his hair. Christie's admiration was palpable, and Wessex (Hardy's name for Dorset) was no longer a fiction. The director of "Darling," "Sunday Bloody Sunday," "Marathon Man" and "Midnight Cowboy" knew what he was doing, all right.

In 1969, I got to talk with William Wyler, one of filmdom's most distinguished directors, in his studio office in Hollywood three months before he began filming Jesse Hill Ford's "The Liberation of L.B. Jones" on locations around the author's hometown of Humboldt, TN.

By the time I met Wyler I was an old hand at covering location filming of major movies. Besides those mentioned, I had also spent several days each on Elia Kazan's "A Face in the Crowd" in Piggott, Ark., and Memphis, and several more on his "Wild River" locations on the Hiwassee River in East Tennessee.

Most of the directors I had watched in action — far from Hollywood and the Screen Actors Guild crowd — had routinely auditioned and hired local actors for small speaking parts, as well as extras for color and background action.

Not Wyler.

I brought up the subject, thinking there might be bit parts in "Liberation of L.B.Jones" for Memphis actors. He was adamant about hiring all of his actors in Hollywood.

"I like to use actors to do the acting, you know," he said laconically. "It's not something you can just pick up overnight. I just don't believe in the anti-acting school. Oh, occasionally you find somebody who's got a marvelous face and you want to photograph him, and you give him a bit. You have him look around or have some kind of reaction, but that's not acting, you know. He's just playing himself. Acting is being somebody else, putting yourself in somebody else's skin and thinking like him."

O.K. It was Wyler talking, so you had to respect his opinions even if you didn't necessarily agree with him.

After all, he had made "Wuthering Heights," "Roman Holiday," "The Best Years of Our Lives," and "Ben-Hur," among many fine films, not to mention the great World War II Air Force documentary, "The Memphis Belle."

He told me he was attracted to "The Liberation of L.B. Jones" because it was such a good story. "Good stories are hard to come by these days," he said. "Plus the fact that it's about something important, something that's happening now." (It was a story of complex race relations in the middle of the Civil Rights struggle.) "Also," he added, "it has good characters and first-class writing. You raise good authors there in Tennessee."

Alas, the film, when it was released in 1970, lacked the passion that had made the novel so much more than a tract on race relations. As I had watched him work on location, Wyler seemed so calm and methodical — almost mechanical, in fact — that I couldn't see the anger and desperation I thought some of the scenes required. And sure enough, in the finished film those emotions, for the most part, simply weren't there. Sadly, it was Wyler's last film, though he lived another decade in retirement.

James Bridges, a fine young writer-director who was my friend from 1977 until his death from cancer in 1993 at the age of 57, did not share Wyler's convictions about using only Hollywood actors when he shot his films on location.

For one of the first films he directed, "9/30/55" (re-titled "Sept. 30, 1955" in later release, and "24 Hours of the Rebel" for TV), virtually every actor in the film, except for the two leads, Richard Thomas and Susan Tyrell, was local talent he found in Conway, Ark.

The offbeat, touching, and generally underrated film, whose title referred to the date screen idol James Dean crashed his Porsche and died, was autobiographical.

"I remember exactly where I was and what I was doing when I heard the awful news about Dean," Bridges told me in our first interview. "I was standing on a ladder adjusting a scenery flat on the stage at Arkansas State Teachers College in Conway. Somebody passed me with a portable radio and I heard fleetingly something about 'Dean' and 'killed.' I slid down the ladder and raced to the campus radio studio to get the details."

Twenty years later, drawing on his own memories, feelings and experiences, Bridges wrote his screenplay about "the day James Dean died," eventually selling it — and himself as director — to Universal.

Like Jimmy J., the hero of his film (brought to life by Richard Thomas in one of his finest performances), Bridges was an Arkansan, who lived in Paris, and went to college in Conway. And, like Jimmy J., he dropped out of school at 18 and followed his dream of being another James Dean to Hollywood.

"It was tough," Bridges said with a rueful smile, "and when I got in to see Dean's agent, Dick Clayton, I still remember vividly how he advised me to go back home. Now

Clayton calls me, and tries to persuade me to put his stars into my pictures."

He ignored Clayton's advice, obviously, and within a couple of years had played roles in about 50 TV shows. But he saw that he wasn't going to become a movie star and started to write and eventually direct. He became a protégé of the UCLA Theatre Group's famed director-producer John Houseman, who later won an Oscar for the role Bridges wrote for him in his film, "The Paper Chase," the screenplay for which also won Bridges an Oscar nomination.

The young director's empathy with actors gave his films an edge that appealed to audiences in the '70s and early '80s. One of his biggest hits, "Urban Cowboy," filmed on locations around Houston, was dead on in its depiction of beer-drinking, games-playing, line-dancing boomers of the era. Actors signed up on location, many of them regulars at Gilly's, the roadhouse where the film's honkytonk interiors were shot, helped establish the film's authenticity. And Bridges got two of their best performances out of Debra Winger and John Travolta.

I was in L.A. a week or so after the premiere of Bridges' other huge hit, "The China Syndrome," and got a call from the excited, incredulous director the day after the Three-Mile Island nuclear power plant meltdown.

"I swear we had nothing to do with it," he told me." But can you believe this?"

The year before, my wife and I had been on one of the hush-hush film's locations with Bridges out in the San Fernando Valley, where the Golden State Freeway passes over Paxton Ave. The sun was shining for the first time in more than a week, and Jim said he was hoping for two more sunny days in a row so he could finish up Jack Lemmon's scenes before the actor had to head East.

I had to promise Bridges I wouldn't write about the film itself — then called "Power" — for fear some TV producer would steal the timely and volatile subject matter and beat them to the punch with a quickie TV show. Instead, I interviewed Lemmon, between takes, about his upcoming Broadway play, "Tribute," his first in 17 years.

A year later at the film's Dallas premiere, Lemmon told me he thought one reason the film in which he co-starred with Jane Fonda and Michael Douglas, came out so well was that Bridges "let me shape the character." He said one of Bridges' great virtues was that "he doesn't over-direct. He's like a good golf pro. Instead of giving you 15 different things to remember, he gives you one clear statement."

I didn't know it at the time, but the last time I saw him at the Bel-Air Hotel in L.A. in 1992, Bridges had been fighting cancer for two years, and would die a year later. He hadn't done anything since the disappointing "Mike's Murder" (1984) and "Bright Lights, Big City," in 1988, and he was clearly depressed that last time I saw him.

"I don't want to do any of the things I'm offered," he said, "and I can't get anybody interested in the original script I want to do."

On a happier note, Mel Brooks, the madcap writer-director of such comedy hits as "The Producers," "The 12 Chairs," "Blazing Saddles," "Young Frankenstein," and "Silent Movie," was high on laughter when I interviewed him in Miami in 1978 the day after the premiere of his Hitchcockian parody, "High Anxiety."

"Even more glorious than the laughter I see on audiences' faces when I sneak in, sit on the front row of a theatre that's playing one of my films, and look back," he told me, "is seeing that they're engrossed. They're transported, with a strange halo of light around their faces, reflected from the screen. It's wonderful. I think, more than anything, that's why I make films."

Brooks recounted writing his first German professor sketch for Sid Caesar on TV's "Show of Shows:" "I was a kid. I was 21. We did the show at the International Theatre on Columbus Circle in New York — 800, maybe 900 seats —and the people all screamed at once at one certain joke.

"For the first time, I was aware of that incredible power! What a power! To make 900 people respond as one. And what noise! To get so much noise out of people! I think I was hooked from that day on. It was terrific."

Warming to his subject, Brooks exulted: "I am flying the banners of insanity for mankind! I'm really into how mankind has behaved, is behaving and will behave. That's why psychiatry is so interesting. I strike out a lot because I swing from the bottom of the bat. Sometimes something like the bean scene from 'Blazing Saddles' can be construed as horribly vulgar, you know."

Brooks admitted that scene could be offensive?

"It could be," he grinned. "To more sensitive souls. Yeah! But I think the world needs somebody like me to be its anarchistic spokesman. It needs somebody to be outrageous. The Marx Brothers used to do it splendidly, but nobody was doing it since, so I thought I might as well take the job."

The middle name of the suave, sophisticated, Cary

Grant-type character he played in "High Anxiety," by the way, is Dr. Richard Harpo Thorndyke. And did I mention that Brooks also co-authored, directed, produced, and wrote the film's title song?

Although he hadn't been able to get a film project off the ground for years, Brooks roared back in 2001 with a Broadway musical version of his 1967 cult film classic, "The Producers," breaking box office records and grabbing every Tony in sight. This time he wrote the whole score!

Elia Kazan in 1999, at the age of 89, was very properly presented an honorary Academy Award for his lifetime achievement. It stirred controversy because at the height of the House Unamerican Activities Committee's hearings into alleged Communist activity in Hollywood in 1952, Kazan, a converted former Communist sympathizer himself, had named names of some other film folk who he said had been duped, as he was, into supporting Communist causes.

In 1997, the Los Angeles Film Critics Association had rejected proposals to give Kazan its lifetime achievement award. The association's vice president, Joseph McBride, told The New York Times that he and his fellow critics judged Kazan on his "morality."

"When you're honoring someone's entire career you're honoring the totality of what he represents.... To give our highest award to him would be ignoring a serious moral issue. We would be passively saying, 'We don't care if people inform on their colleagues.'"

So what did the L.A. critics do? They gave their lifetime achievement award to Roger Corman, director of such screen classics as "Attack of the Crab Monsters," "A Bucket of Blood,"

"Swamp Women," and "Man With the X-Ray Eyes."

Kazan's film output, by contrast, has included "East of Eden," which made a star of James Dean; "A Face in the Crowd," which starred Patricia Neal and a countrified newcomer named Andy Griffith; Tennessee Williams' "A Streetcar Named Desire," which made a screen star of Marlon Brando and won Oscars for Vivien Leigh, Karl Malden and Kim Hunter; Budd Schulberg's "On the Waterfront," which won Oscars for best film and best direction as well as best actor for Brando and best supporting actress for Eva Marie Saint; "Gentlemen's Agreement," which won best picture and best direction Oscars for Kazan; "Panic in the Streets," filmed on location in New Orleans, and generally credited with moving filmmaking off Hollywood sound stages and out into the real world; "Wild River," and "The Arrangement."

I interviewed Kazan several times over the years, watched him at work on three of his films between 1956 and 1969, and got to know him well enough to be pretty sure he got his biggest laugh in years over being beaten out for this L.A. critics' "honor" by Roger Corman.

The film and theatre communities had long since forgiven Kazan for his 1952 HUAC testimony. Arthur Miller, one of those whose names Kazan named, chose him in 1954 to direct the premiere production of his confessional drama, "After the Fall." And in 1955, the Motion Picture Academy voted him best-picture and best-direction Oscars for "On the Waterfront."

Kazan's films were always mesmerizing to watch, and I found watching him work just as fascinating. His actors were often in awe of him, and at times I'm sure they hated him, because he would do anything he felt he had to do to arouse the

Director Elia Kazan, stripped for action on location for 1957's "A Face in the Crowd." (Author's collection)

particular emotions he wanted to see them project on the screen.

At the end of my first day as an observer on the Piggott, Ark., locations for "A Face in the Crowd" in 1956, I was going to drive my old Knoxville, TN, schoolmate, Patricia Neal, to a hotel in nearby Kennett, Mo., for dinner. She asked if fellow cast members Andy Griffith and Anthony Franciosa could go along. The catered food on location had all three of them craving a good square meal, and Franciosa's ulcer was acting up.

Going and coming in my station wagon, the

conversation was all about the film — and mostly about "Gadge," as Kazan's associates called him.

Griffith, a monologist unschooled as an actor at that time, and making his film debut, told the following story about

Although director Elia Kazan urged actor Montgomery Clift to let a double be thrown into "Wild River," Clift insisted on doing it himself. (Author's collection)

how Kazan worked:

"I had this scene," he said, "where I was supposed to get furious — you know, just really blow up — and I just couldn't seem to do it. So Gadge called a break but stayed there just talkin' to me about this and that. Somehow he got me to talkin' 'bout when I was in high school back in North Carolina. I told him my family was real poor and all, and literally lived on the wrong side of the tracks.

"Then somehow I found myself tellin' him 'bout this beautiful girl from one of the well-to-do families who I used to see every day in school, and how one day I finally got up enough nerve to ask her for a date but she turned me down.

"He wanted to know why, and I really didn't want to talk about it any more, but he kept after me till I told him what happened, which was that she gave me the most witherin' look I ever got from anybody and then drew herself up and said, 'I don't go out with poor white trash!'

"Well, I'll never forget that moment as long as I live, but I really didn't want to talk about it, so I changed the subject and we talked on a few more minutes. Then he said, 'O.K., Andy, let's try it again.'

"Of course, Gadge sits right under the camera lens when he's directin', and that's where he was when we were doin' this scene. We were shootin' without sound so he could just get this close-up of my angry reaction.

"So he was talkin' to me, tryin' to pull it out of me, and suddenly he said, 'Come on, white trash! I want to see you get mad. Come on, white trash!

"And I'll tell you what. That did it. He got the take he wanted."

But Kazan was also caring and protective of his actors, having been one himself with New York's famed Group Theatre before establishing himself as one of Broadway's greatest directors with such productions as "The Skin of Our Teeth," "One Touch of Venus," "All My Sons," "A Streetcar Named Desire," "Cat on a Hot Tin Roof," and "Death of a Salesman."

On a cold winter day in 1960 on a raftlike float in the Hiwassee River in East Tennessee, where he was filming "Wild River," I watched Kazan beg Montgomery Clift again and again to use a stunt double, who was standing by, instead of allowing himself, as a TVA agent charged with moving people off the land that would become lake bottom when the dam under construction was completed, to be thrown into the near-freezing water by an angry land-owner. Teeth chattering and shoulders shaking, Clift refused, going through the ordeal again and again until Kazan pronounced the scene perfect. And of course the finished film was that much better for Clift's insistence on complete realism.

Marlon Brando evidently picked up Kazan's habit of sitting under the camera lens as he directed. But wait a minute — he was supposed to be just acting in "The Chase" the day I visited the set of that now notorious 1965 film at Columbia.

Yet there he was, making like he was directing the film which Arthur Penn had been hired to direct.

As I approached the sound stage being used for Sam Spiegel's film, with a screenplay by Lillian Hellman, based on a novel and play by Horton Foote, I walked right past a large red-and-white sign on the heavy door which warned "Closed Set — No Exceptions." I walked past it because the unit publicist, Mac St. Johns, had arranged for me to.

"You and Army Archerd (columnist for Variety) are the only newspapermen who've been allowed on the set," he told me. Brando had demanded the closed set because the Hollywood press corps had worked him over a couple of months before during his child custody clash with his former wife, Anna Kashfi. I was not interested in Brando's private life; I just wanted to watch him work.

Shortly after I arrived on the set, Brando emerged from his trailer in the khakis and badge of a contemporary smalltown Texas sheriff. The scene to be shot was a long fight sequence in which three town toughs attack the sheriff in his own office. Part of the fight, in which Brando, his face battered and bloody, is thrown down the courthouse steps, had already been shot, with Brando himself taking the fall down the concrete steps.

This morning, for some reason, Brando had decided to let his stunt double take the fall when he is thrown to the floor of his office by the three toughs.

They rehearsed that part of it, with director Penn watching from one side of the set and Brando watching just as intently from under the camera, Kazan-style. I won't bore you with the endless details, but Brando and Penn got into an argument about how the scene should be played.

They argued back and forth, and forth and back.

Brando: "I don't think this guy would give up that easy..."

Penn: "No. He would realize he had three guys with guns facing him and he would give up, at least temporarily...."

The argument was still going on an hour later when I left the set. I don't remember from the film who won, but if Brando and Penn argued like that over every scene, it's no wonder the film, which also starred Jane Fonda, Robert Redford, E.G. Marshall, Angie Dickinson and Robert Duvall, became one of the biggest bombs in movie history.

About 10 years later, one of Hollywood's legendary directors, King Vidor, who made his first (silent) film in 1919, visited Memphis to speak at a film seminar. In the interview he gave me, the 82-year-old filmmaker bemoaned what he saw happening to filmmaking in Hollywood. And the film he cited as proof of the degradation of the whole process was "The Missouri Breaks," which had reunited that "Chase" team of director Arthur Penn and star Marlon Brando.

Here's what Vidor said about "Missouri Breaks":

"Oh God! That picture made me angry! Marlon Brando playing around, changing his hat and his costume and his accent for every scene. It's a degradation of the whole damn moving picture idea. It looked like he and Jack Nicholson got together and said, let's undermine the director (Penn). It seemed to me obvious. I left the theatre almost nauseated by that film."

How could actors so undermine their director? Here's how Vidor explained the problem: "The No.1 reason I haven't made a film in 17 years is that most of my films were made for big studios where you could deal with one man who made all the decisions. Now they've gone into a promotional thing where you have to get a big star, and that's the key.

"I wasn't good at that and I didn't know anybody who was. You have to sit on stars' doorsteps and cater to them rather than worry about the quality of the screenplay, and let the stars come to you.

"My films sort of grew out of my psyche, most of them.

They were personal statements, and I had to know somebody in charge of a big studio that I could transfer my enthusiasm and my idealism to. Now the agents are running everything, and you end up with packages that the director can't control."

Among the silent classics directed by Vidor are "The Big Parade" and "The Crowd." Then in 1928 he made "Hallelujah!," the second sound musical, filmed, mostly on locations around Memphis, right after "The Jazz Singer." In a career that lasted almost half a century, he also directed "The Citadel," "Stella Dallas," "The Fountainhead," "Duel in the Sun," and, his own favorite, the 1956 "War and Peace," starring Henry Fonda, Audrey Hepburn, Mel Ferrer, Vittorio Gassman, John Mills, and Herbert Lom. In spite of his obvious discouragement over the filmmaking process as it had evolved by the mid-1970s (and largely prevails today), King Vidor declared he was not retired. Even though it was 17 years since his last film, and he was 82 years old, he had a script ready and was looking for a star. He died on his ranch in 1982 at the age of 88. He had never managed to get another film off the ground.

NEED A GIFT? GIVE THIS FASCINATING, FUN-TO-READ
BOOK TO YOUR FAMILY AND FRIENDS!

Yes, I would like to order _____ copies of *Seeing Stars: Memoirs of a Professional Celebrity Seeker* for $24.95 each.
Include $2.95 shipping and handling for one book and $1.95 for each additional book.

# of copies		price per copy		
_____	x	$24.95	=	_____
Virginia Residents please add sales tax of 4.5%			=	_____
Shipping 1st copy	x	$2.95	=	$2.95
Shipping Additional copy	x	$1.95	=	_____
		PAYMENT TOTAL	=	_____

Payment must accompany orders. Please make checks payable to:

Rocky Run Publishing, LLC

Do not send cash. Allow 2 weeks for delivery. If you would like to arrange for expedited delivery, please e-mail RockyRunllc@aol.com

Name: _____

Address: _____

City/State/Zip: _____

Phone: _____E-mail: _____

Please return this form with payment to:

Rocky Run Publishing, LLC
1390 Chain Bridge Road, #230,
McLean, Virginia, 22101

Cut Along Dotted Line and Return